Dreamlings Magical COLORING BOOK

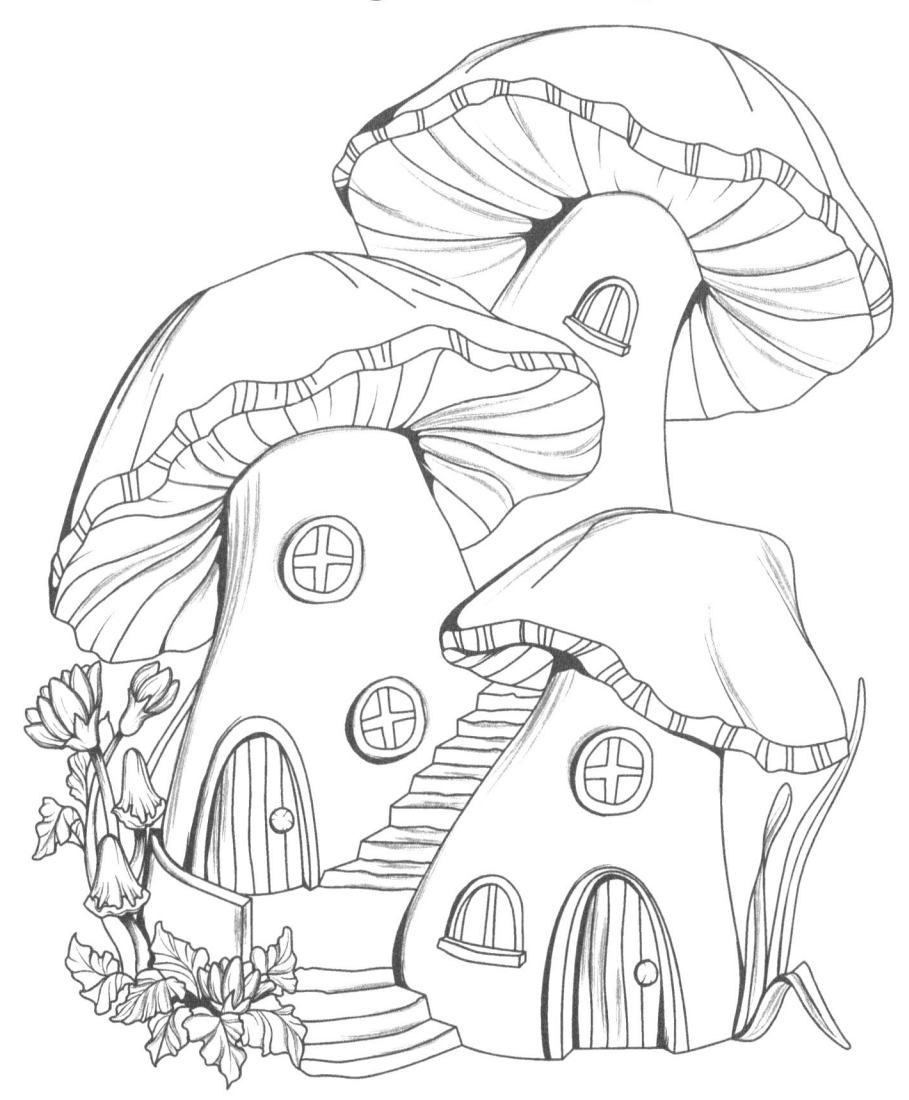

— RUSS FOCUS —

ISBN-13: 978-1724816375   ISBN-10: 1724816373
PUBLISHED BY RUSS FOCUS COPYRIGHT © 2018 ALL RIGHTS RESERVED
NO PART OF THIS PUBLICATION MAY BE REPRODUCED IN ANY
FORM OR BY ANY MEANS WITHOUT WRITTEN PERMISSION OF THE PUBLISHER.
WE ARE NOT RESPONSIBLE FOR UNSOLICITES MATERIAL PUBLISHED IN USA

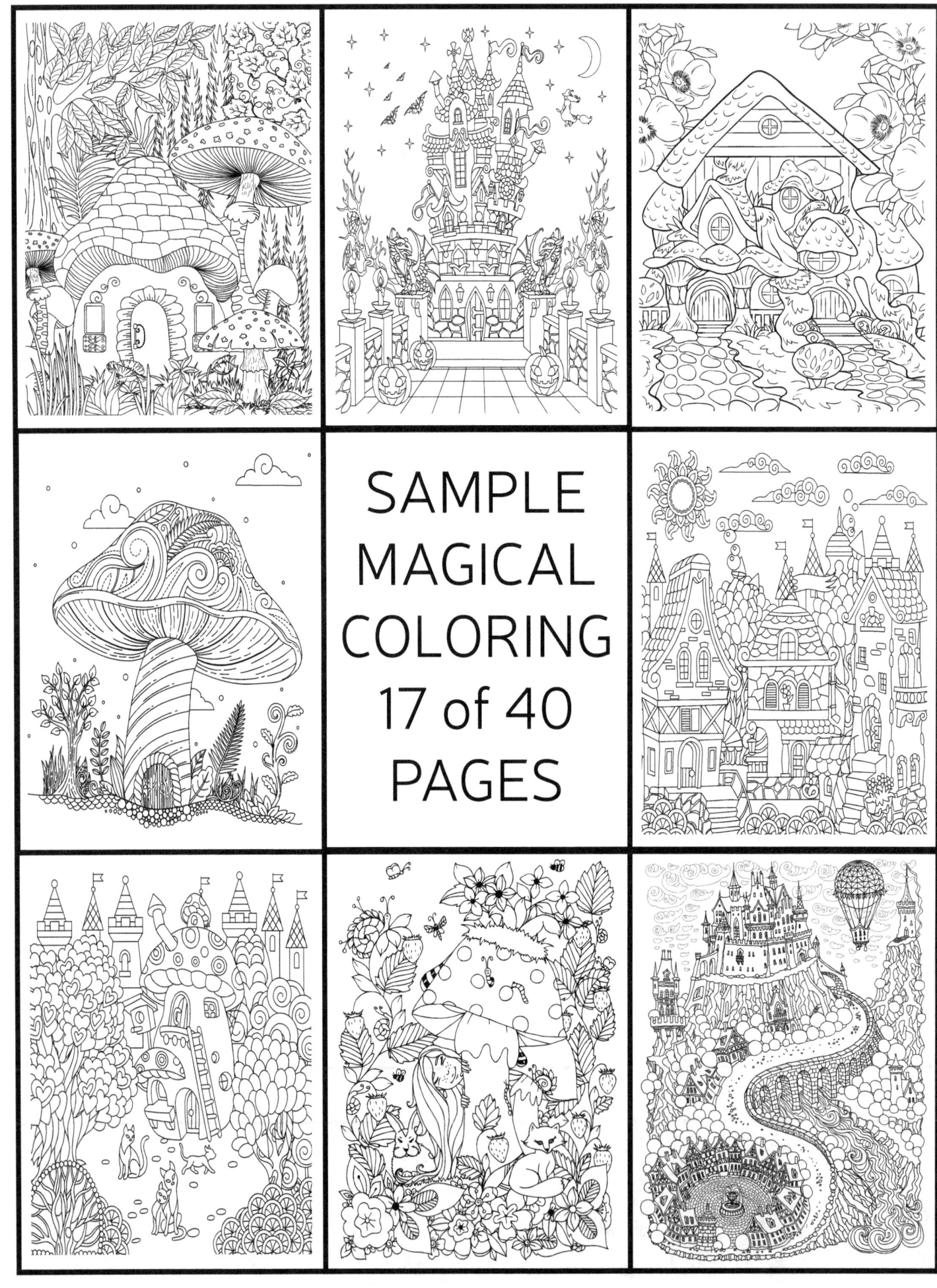

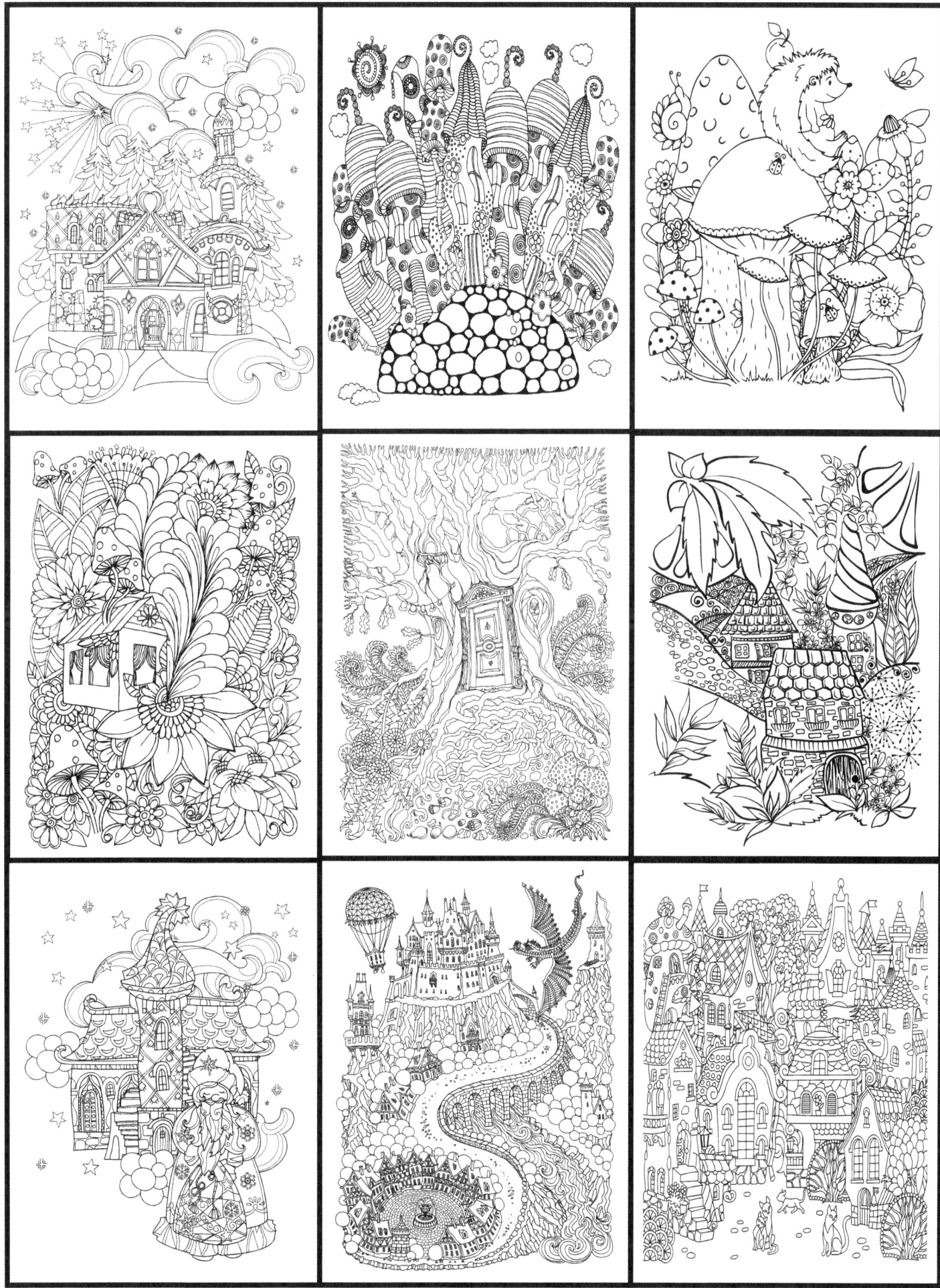

www.russfocus.com

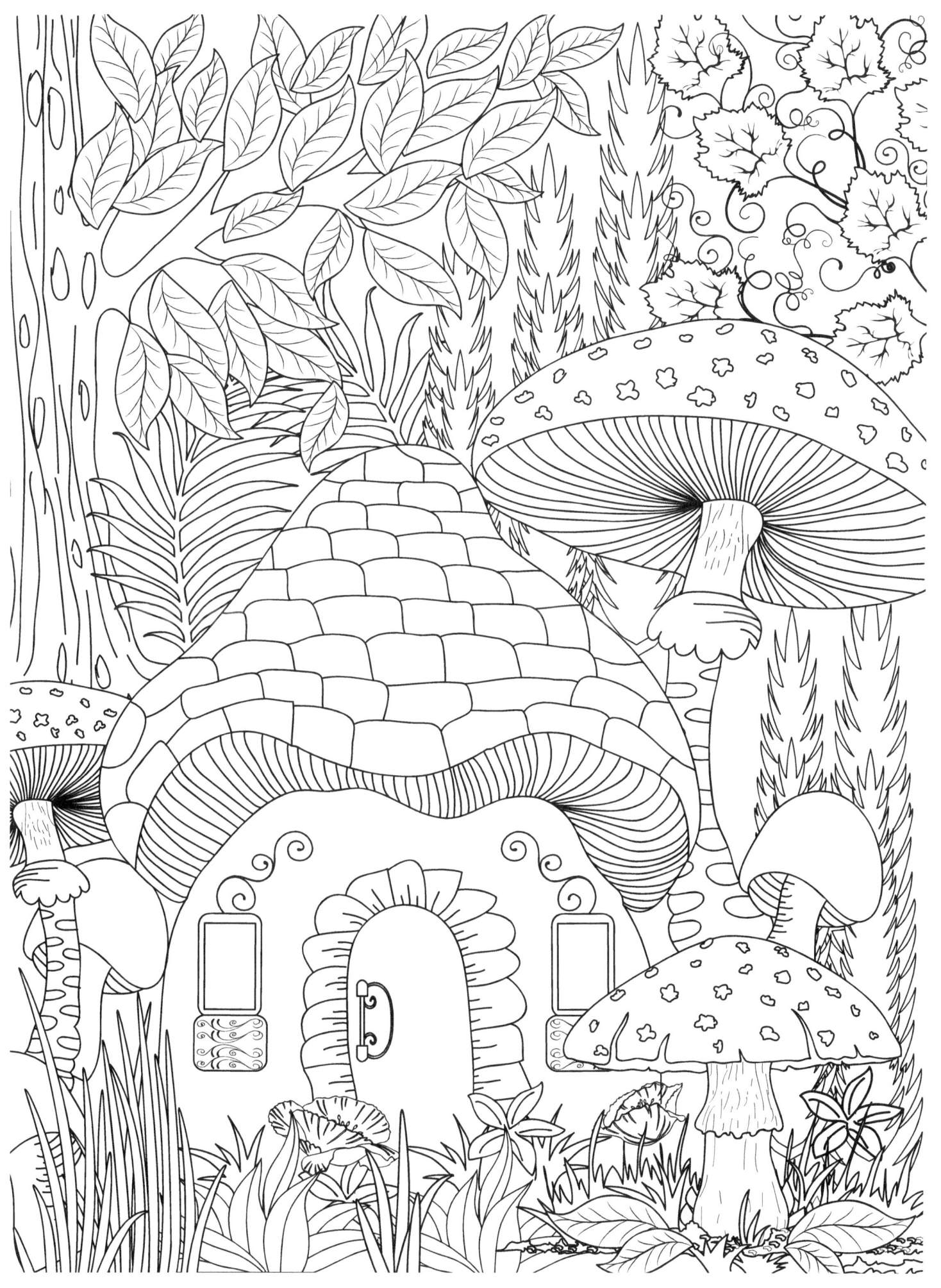

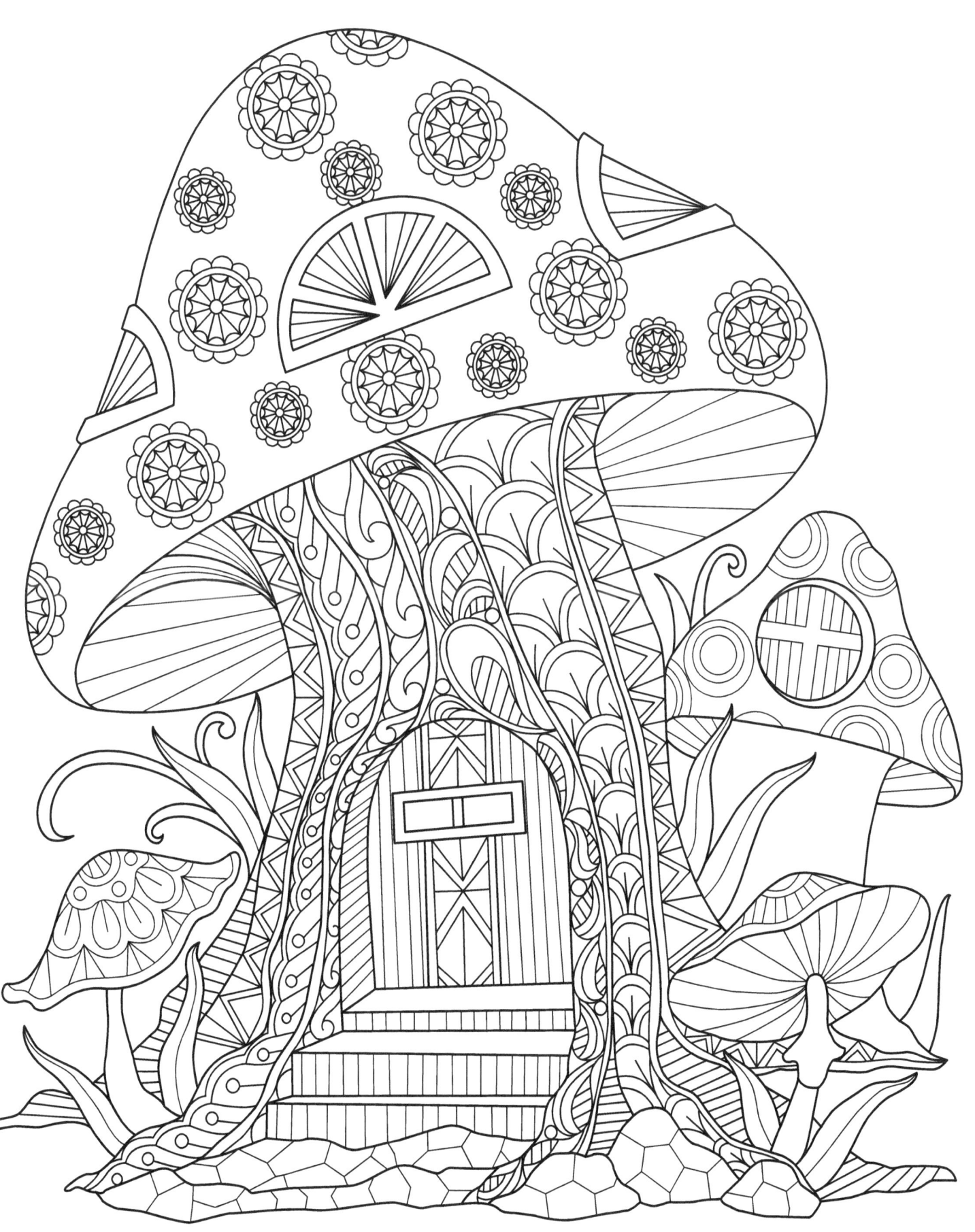

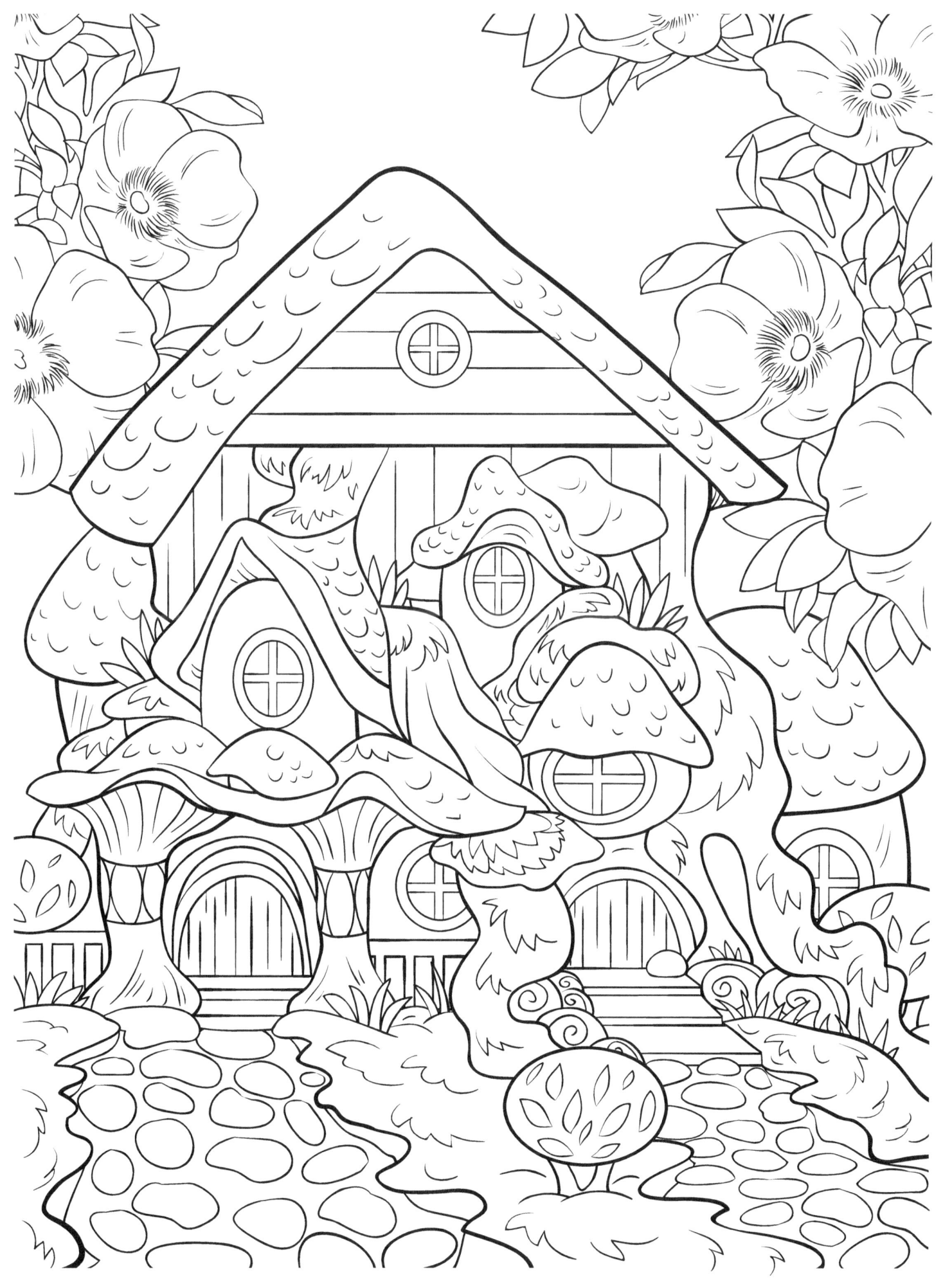

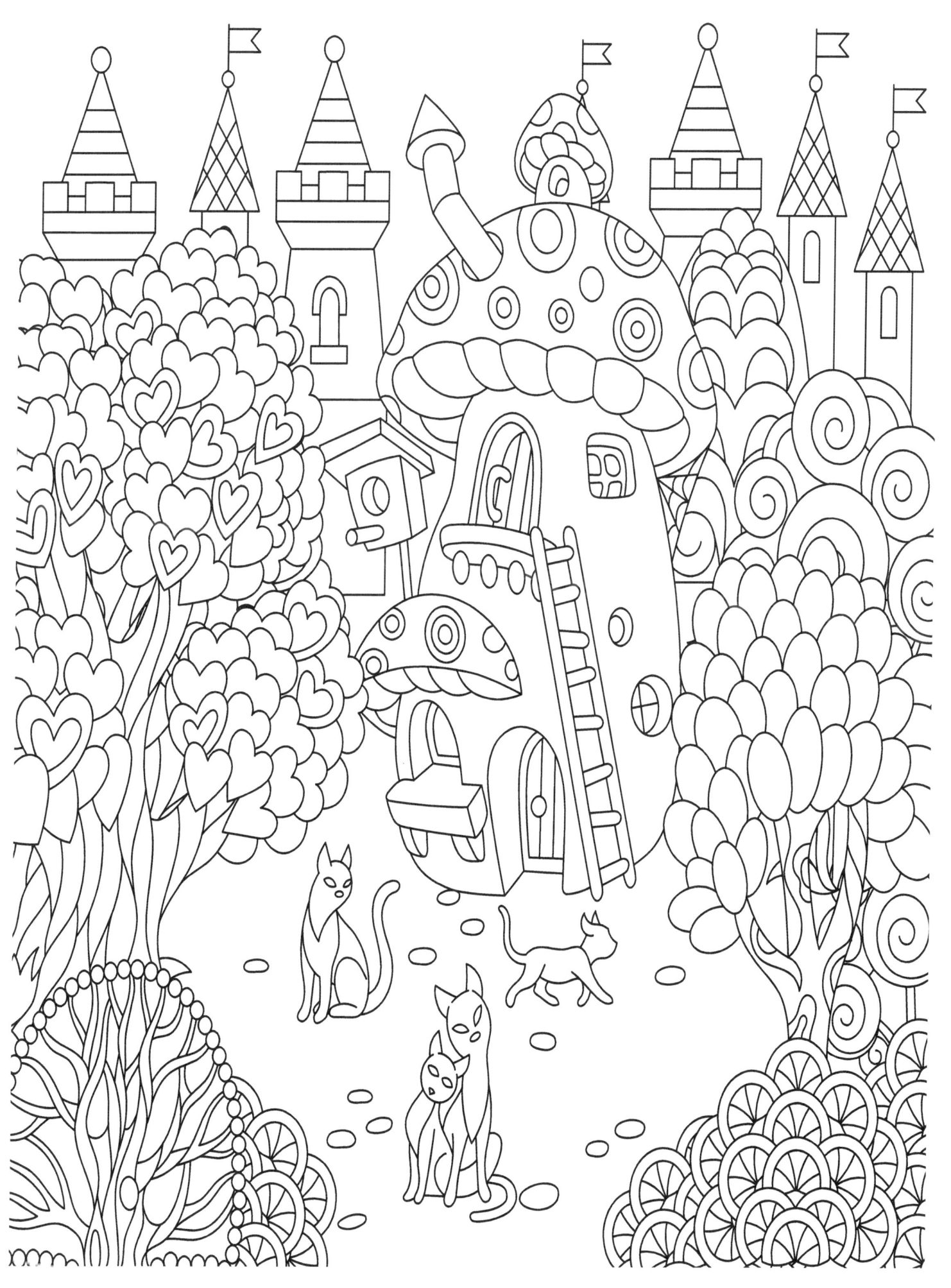

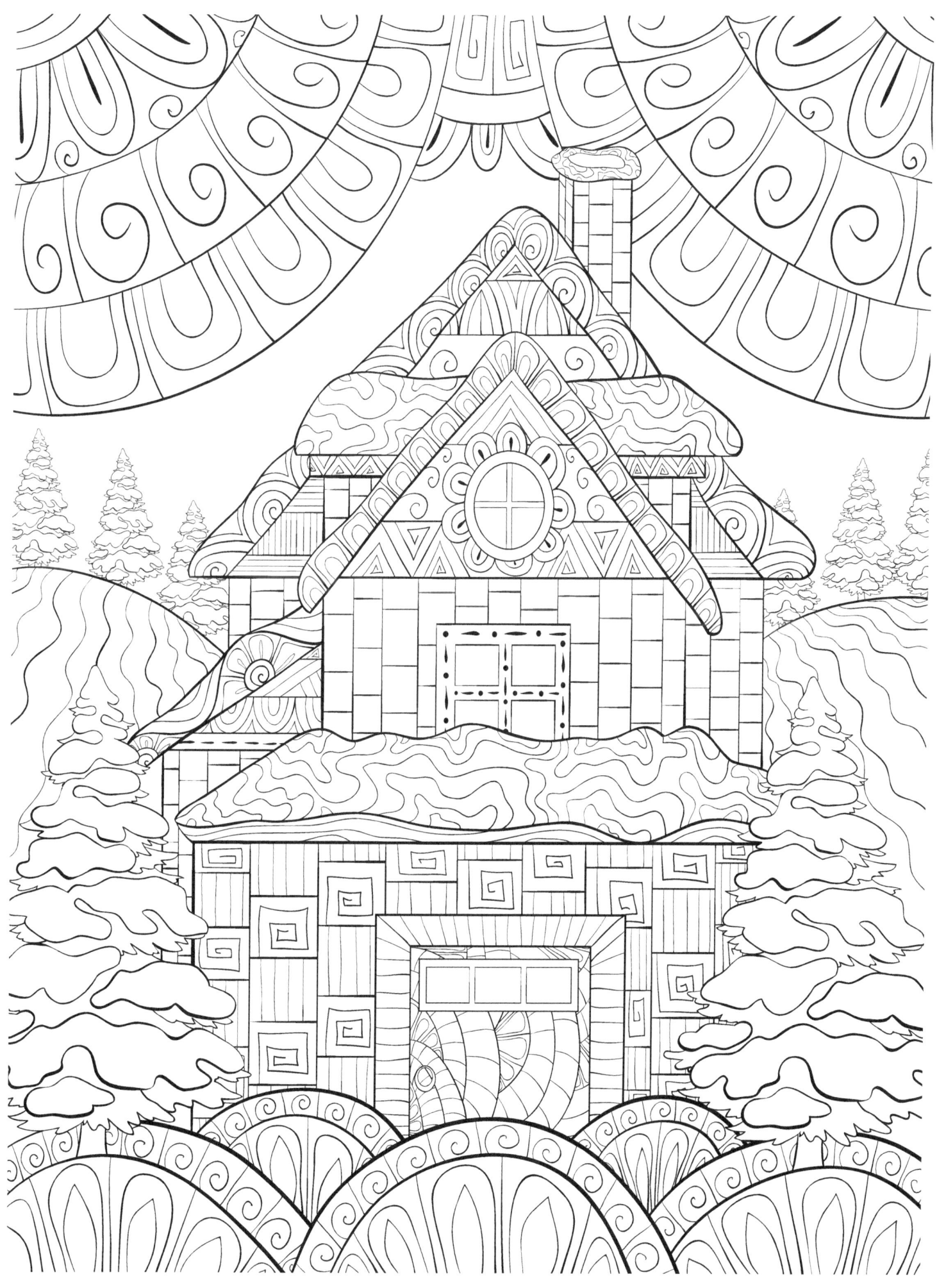

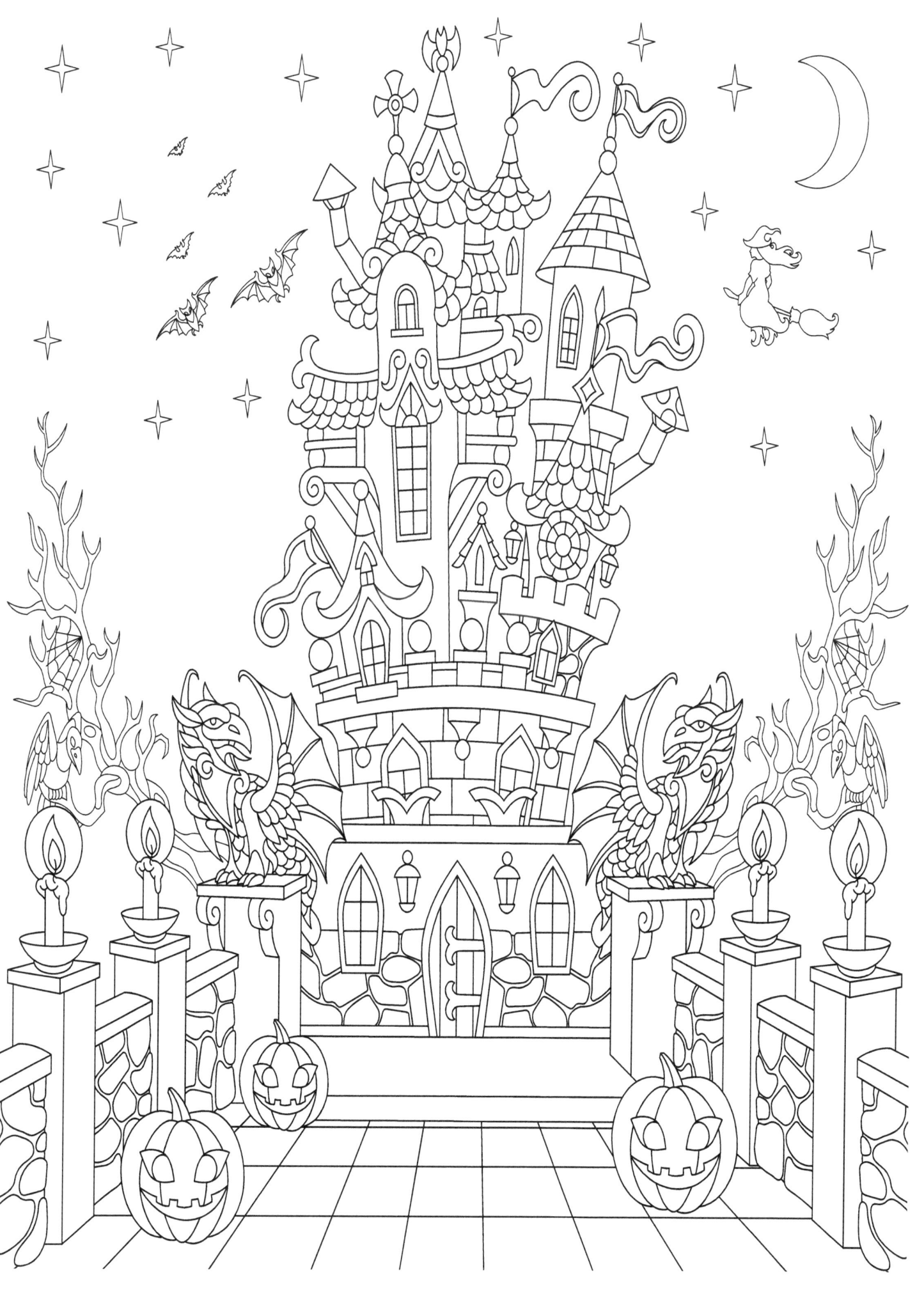

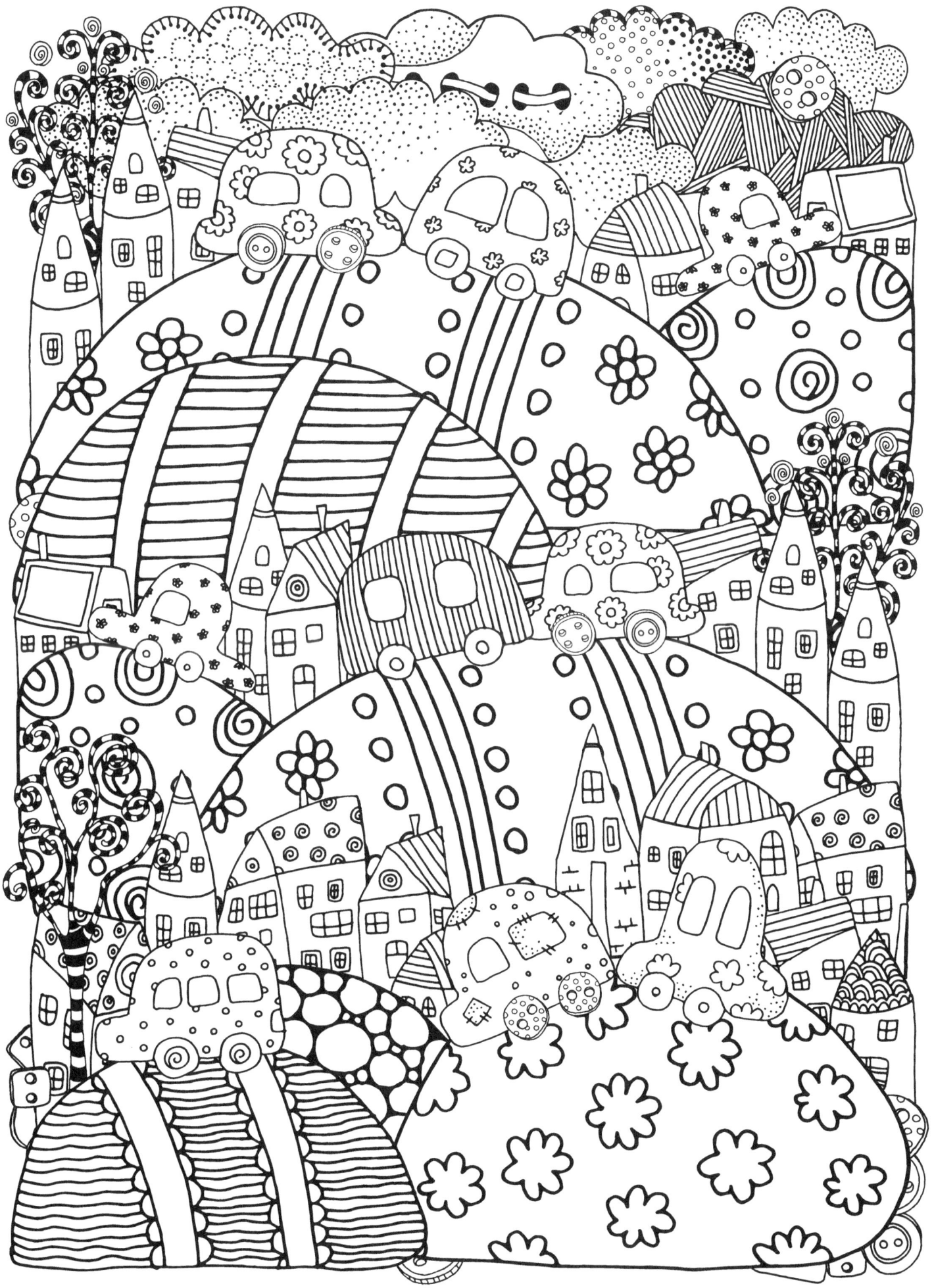

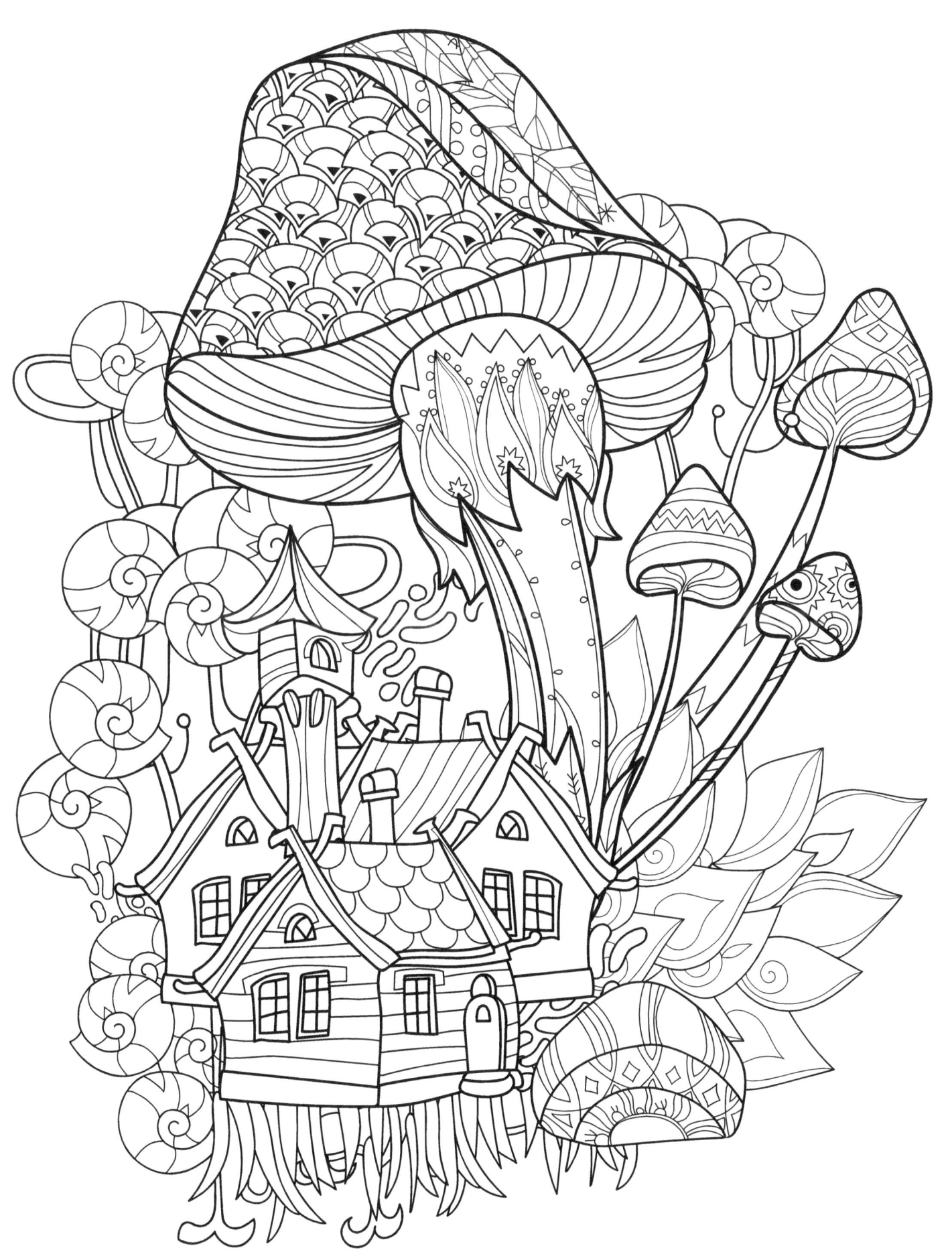

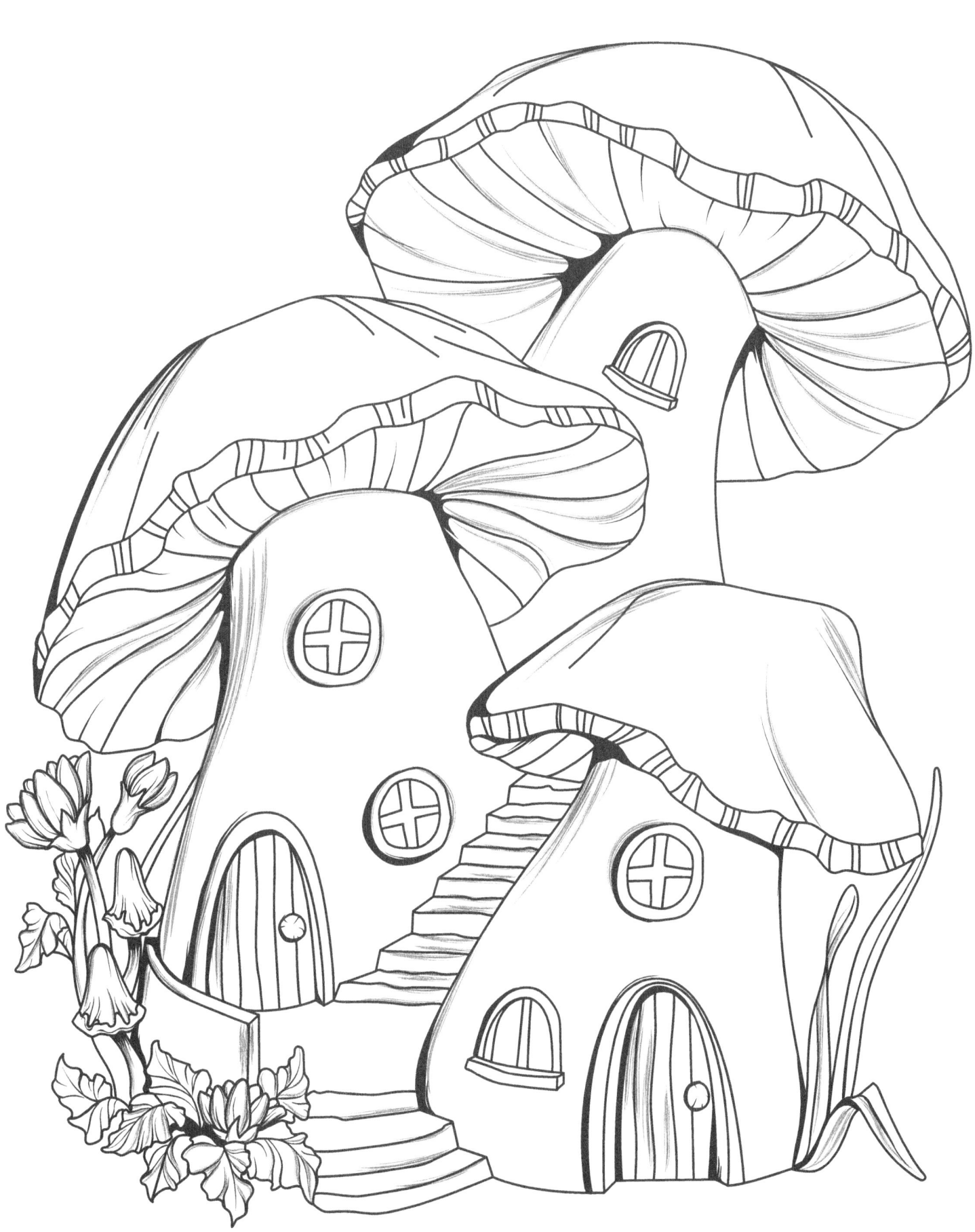

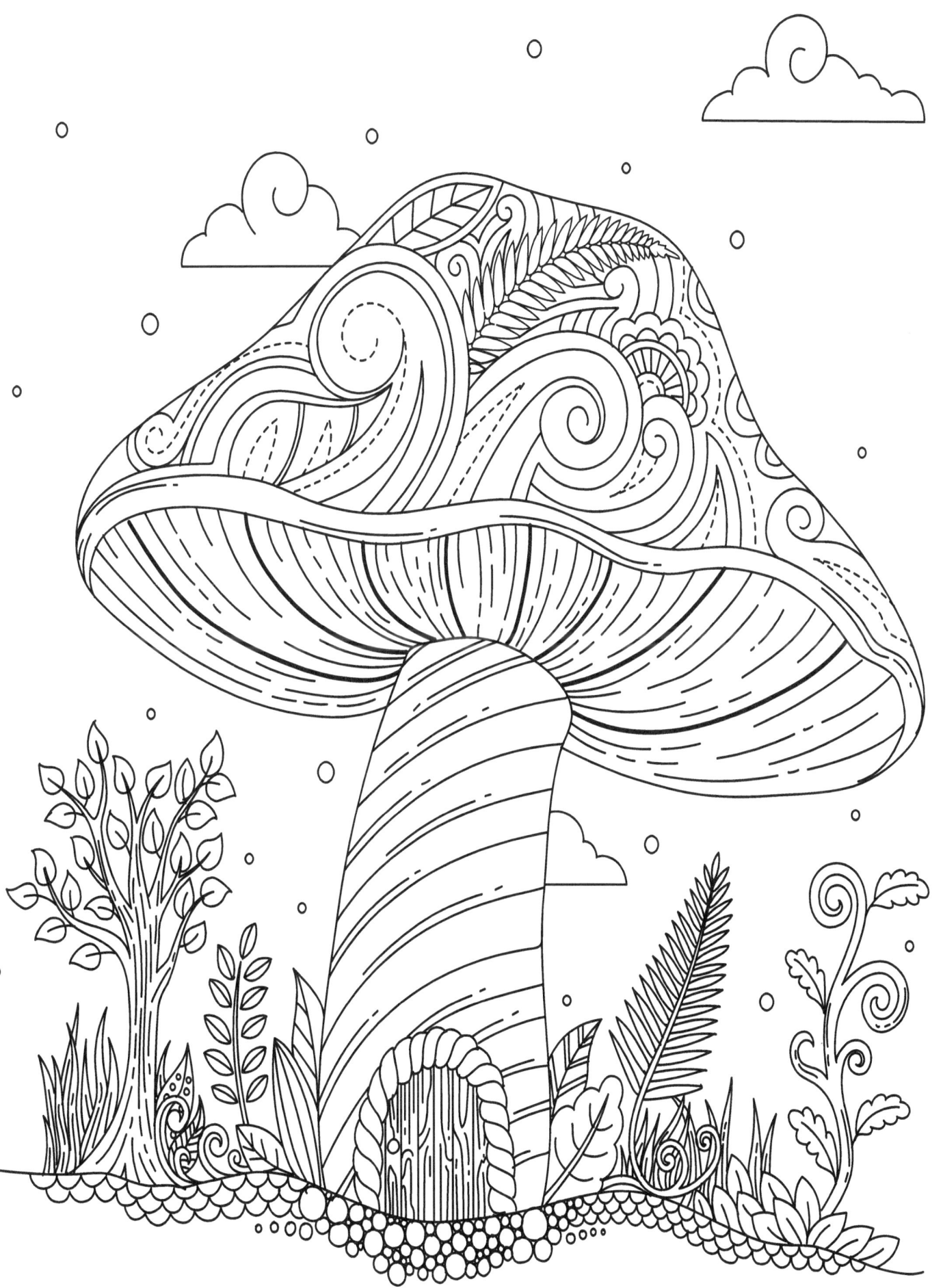

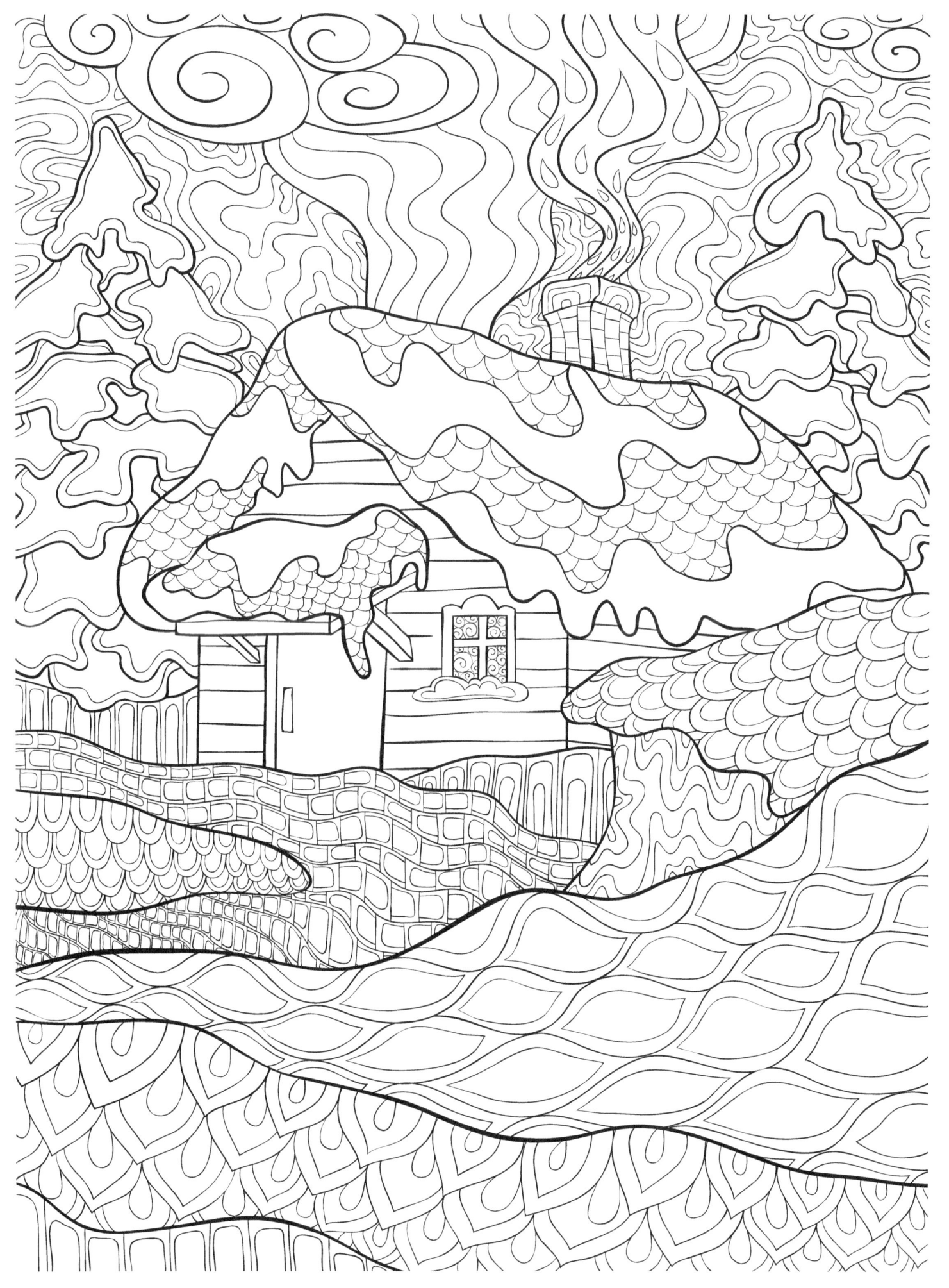

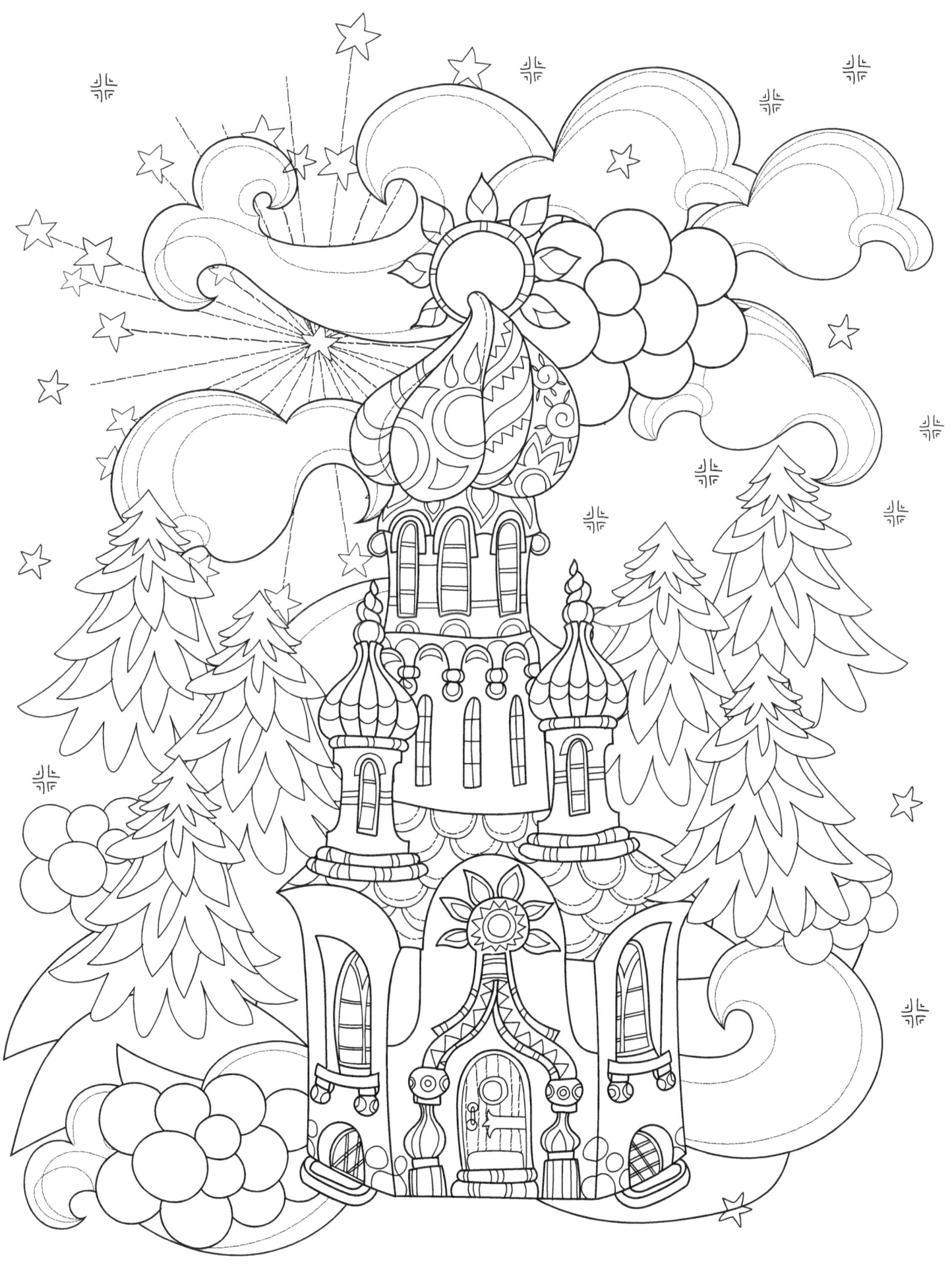

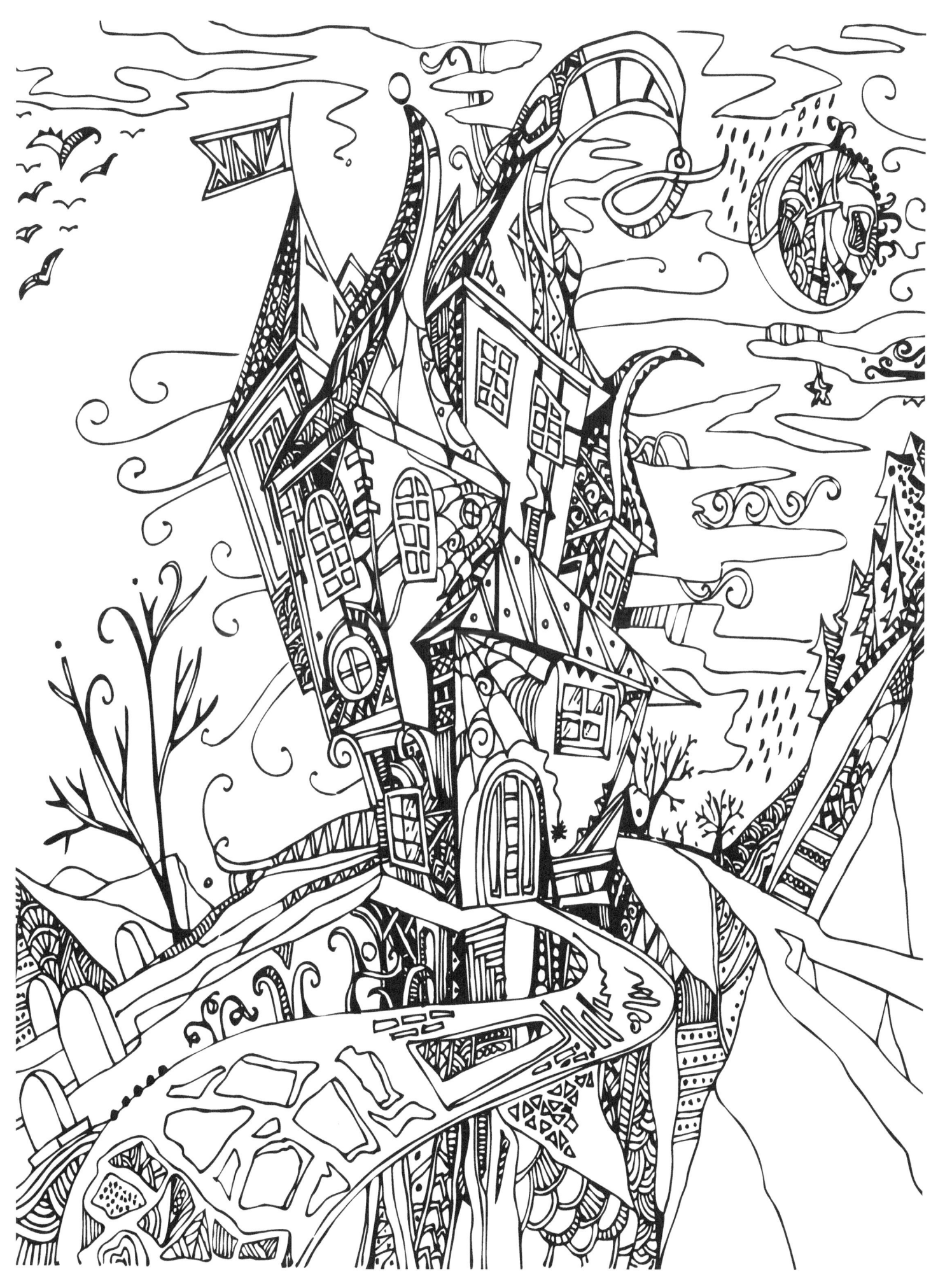

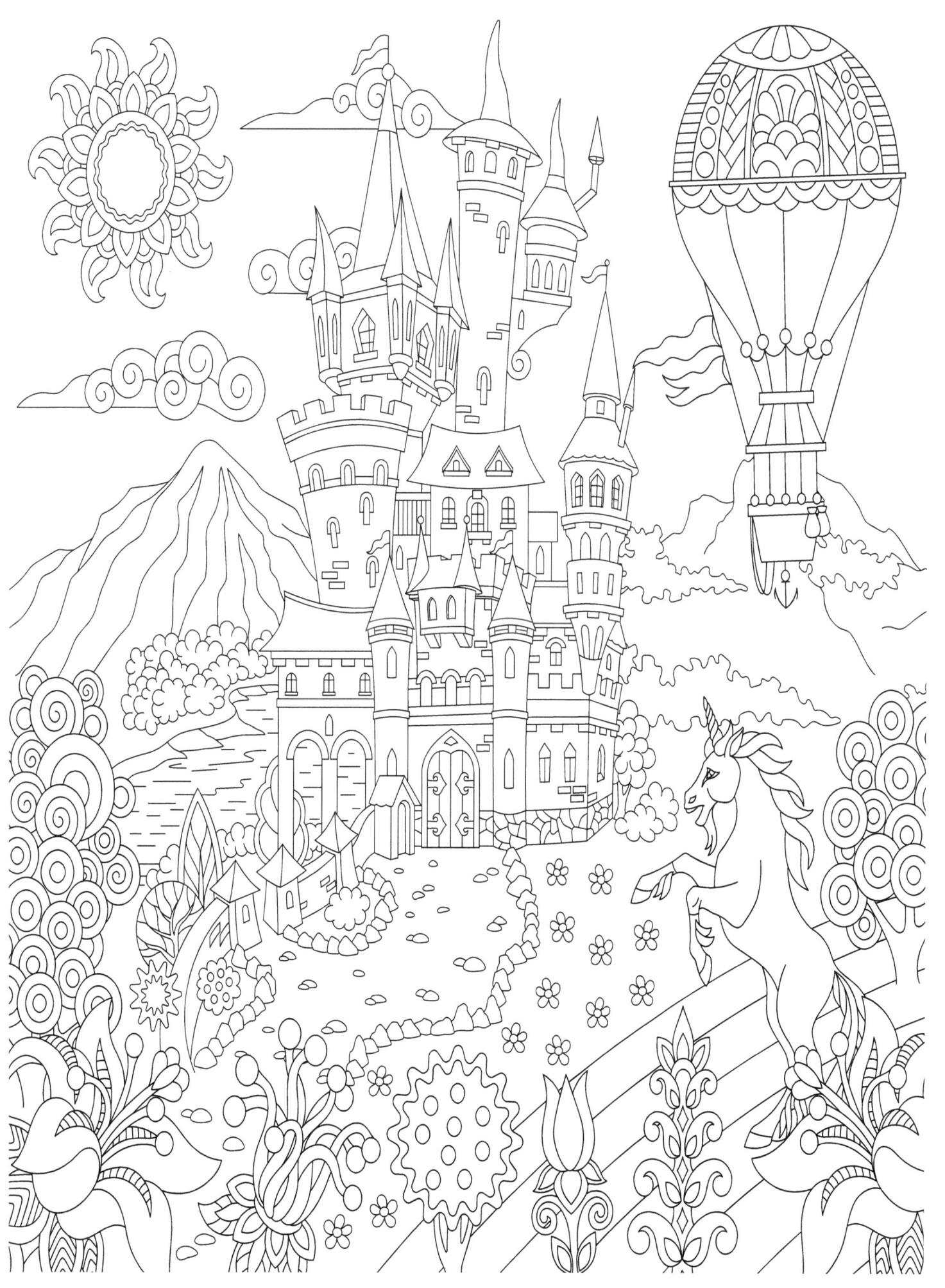

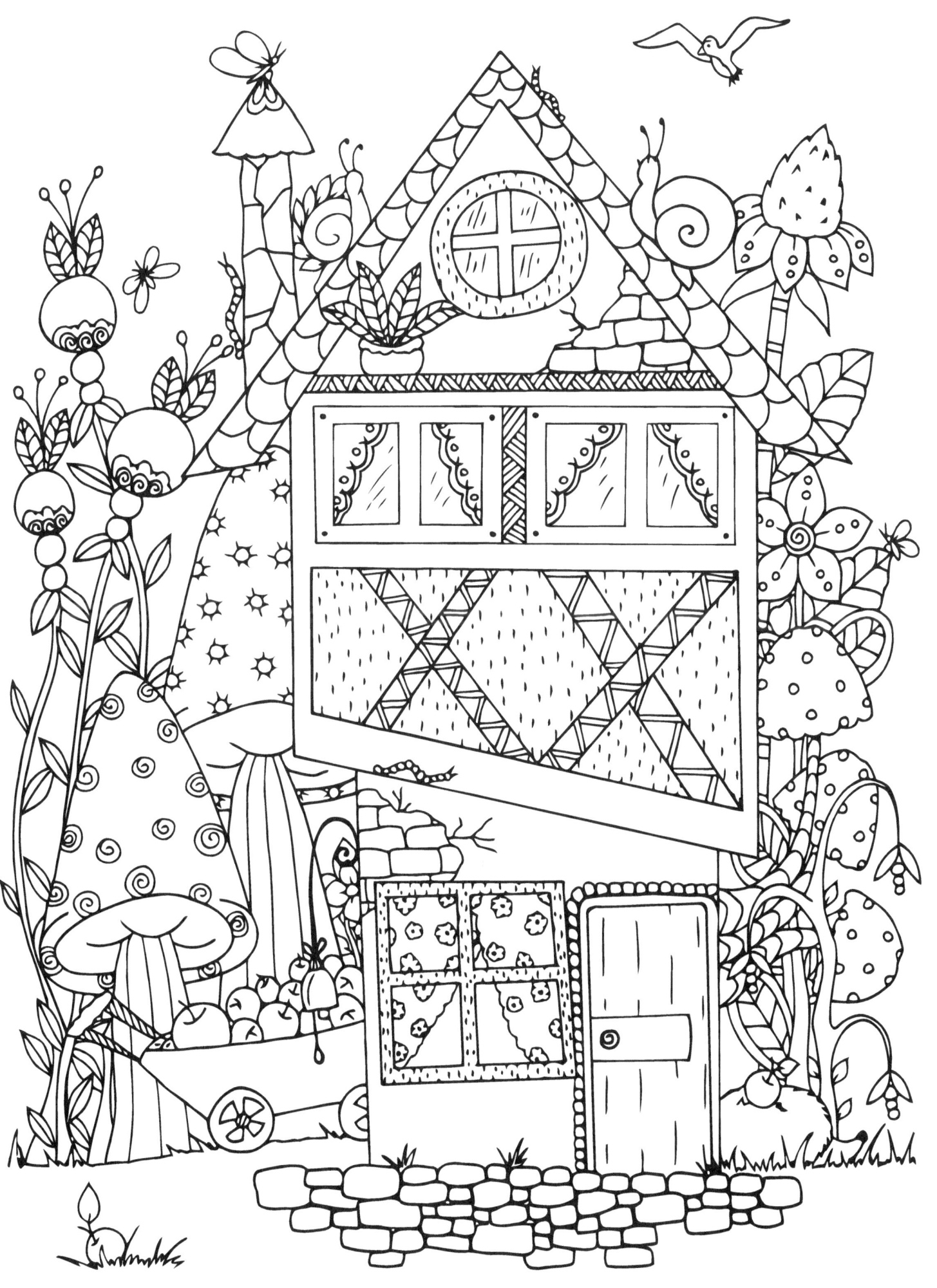

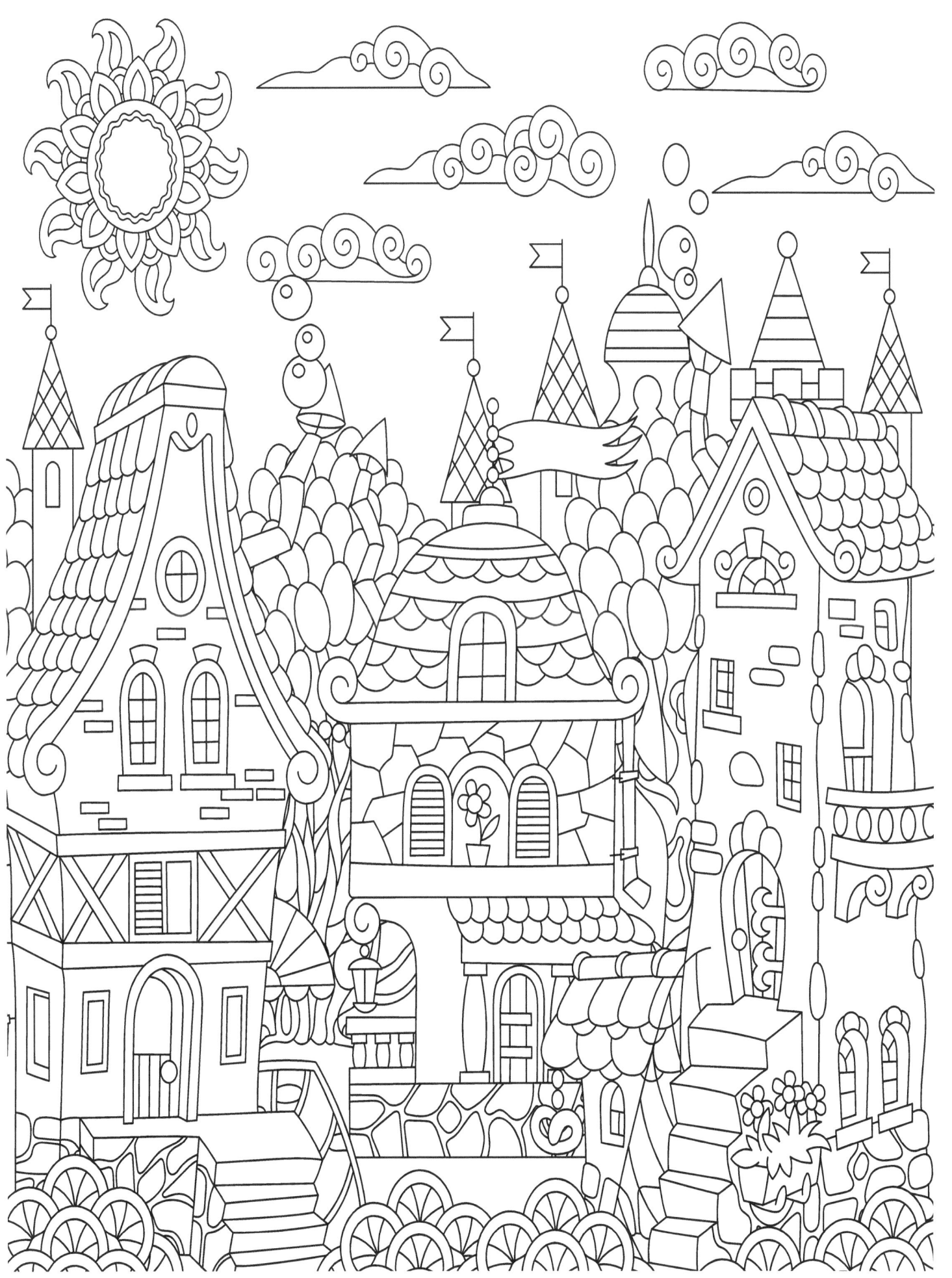

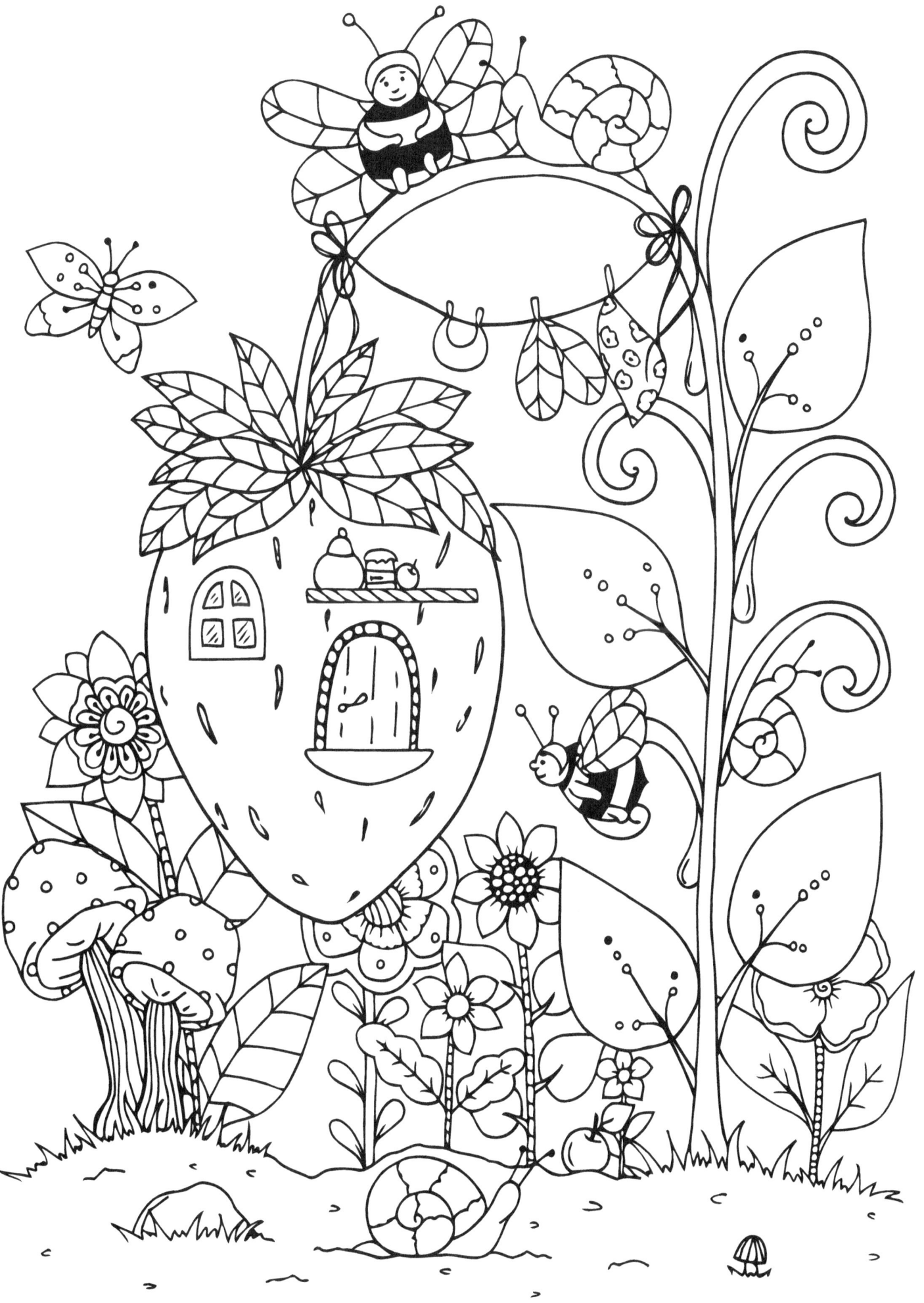

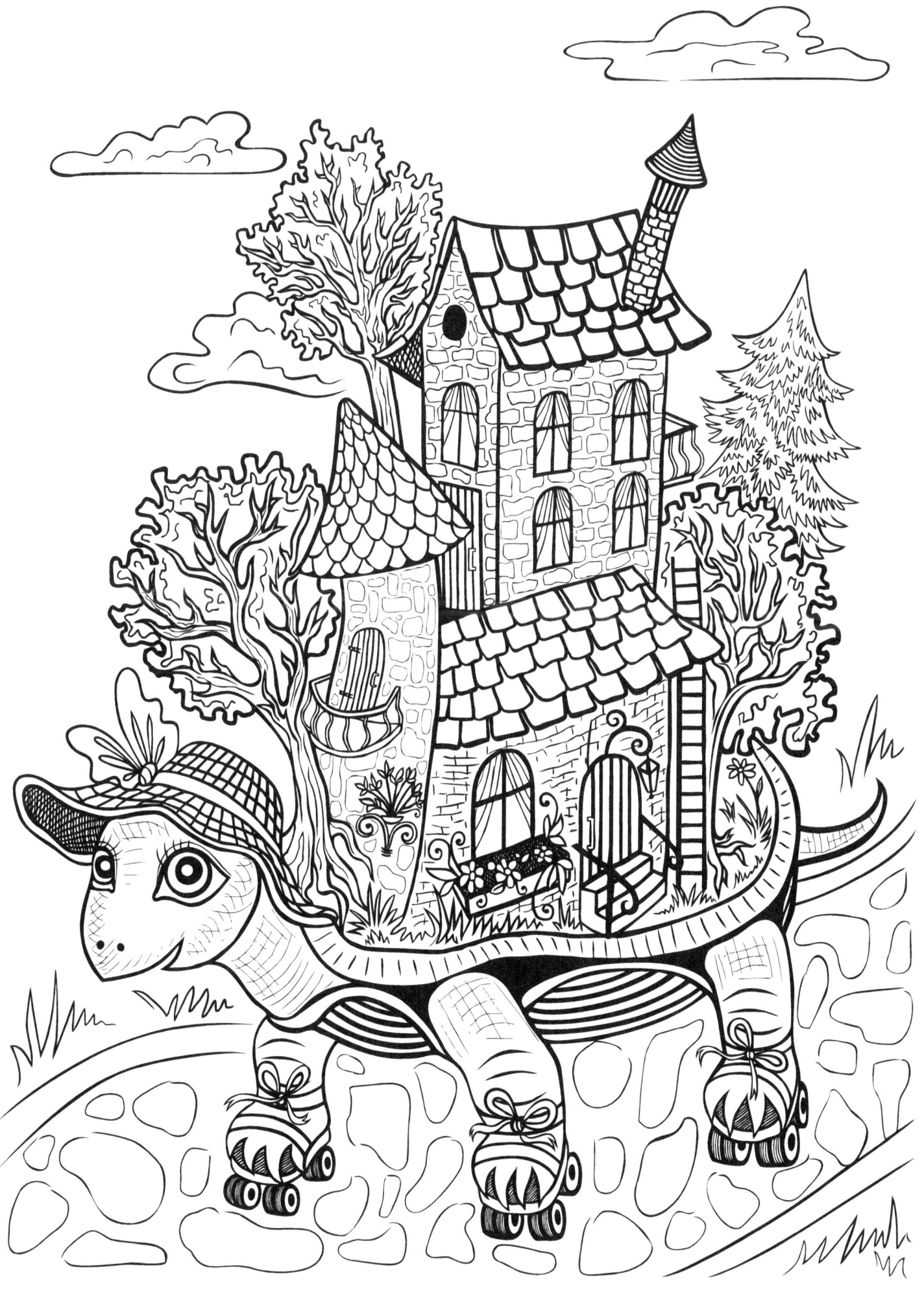

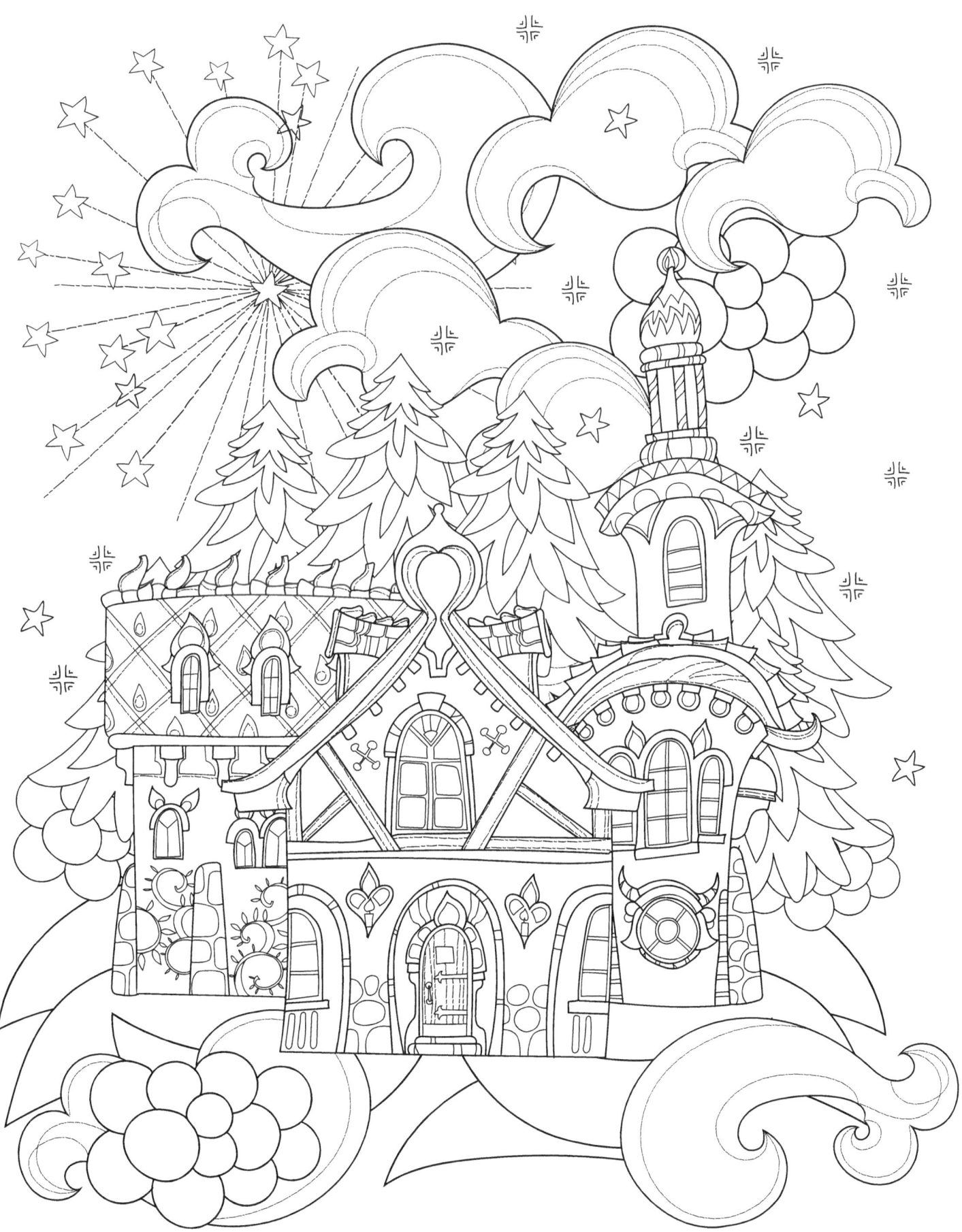

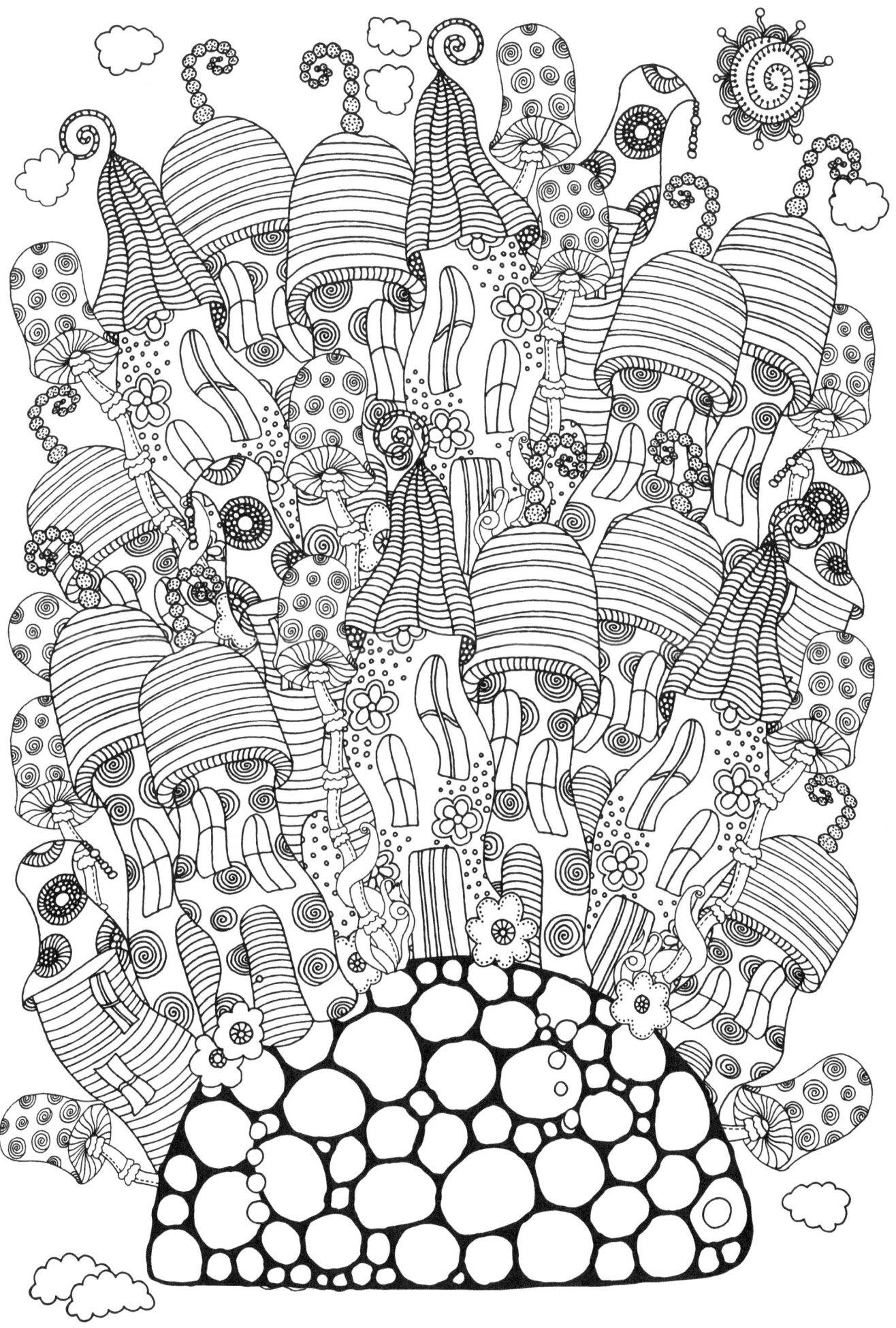

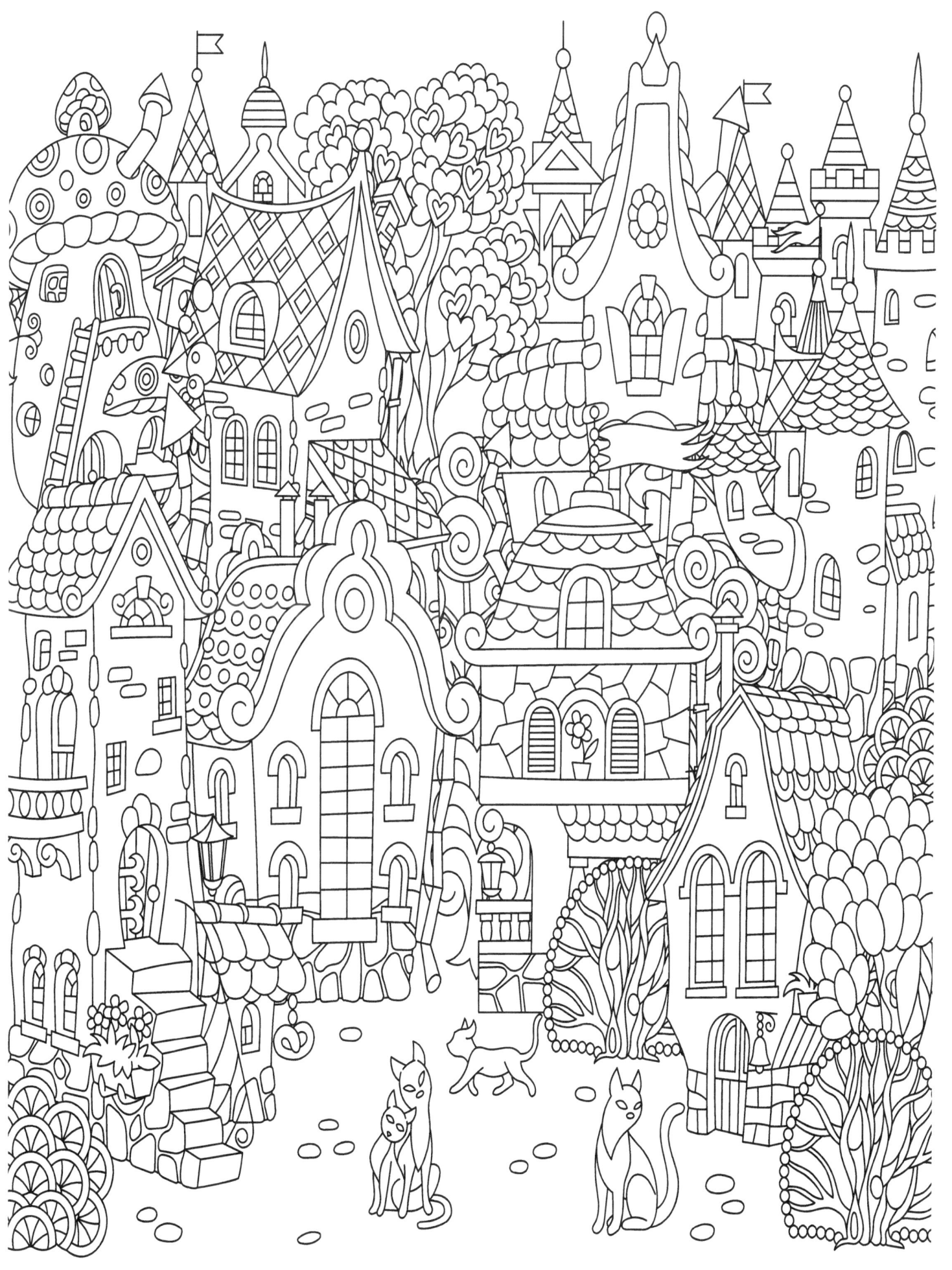

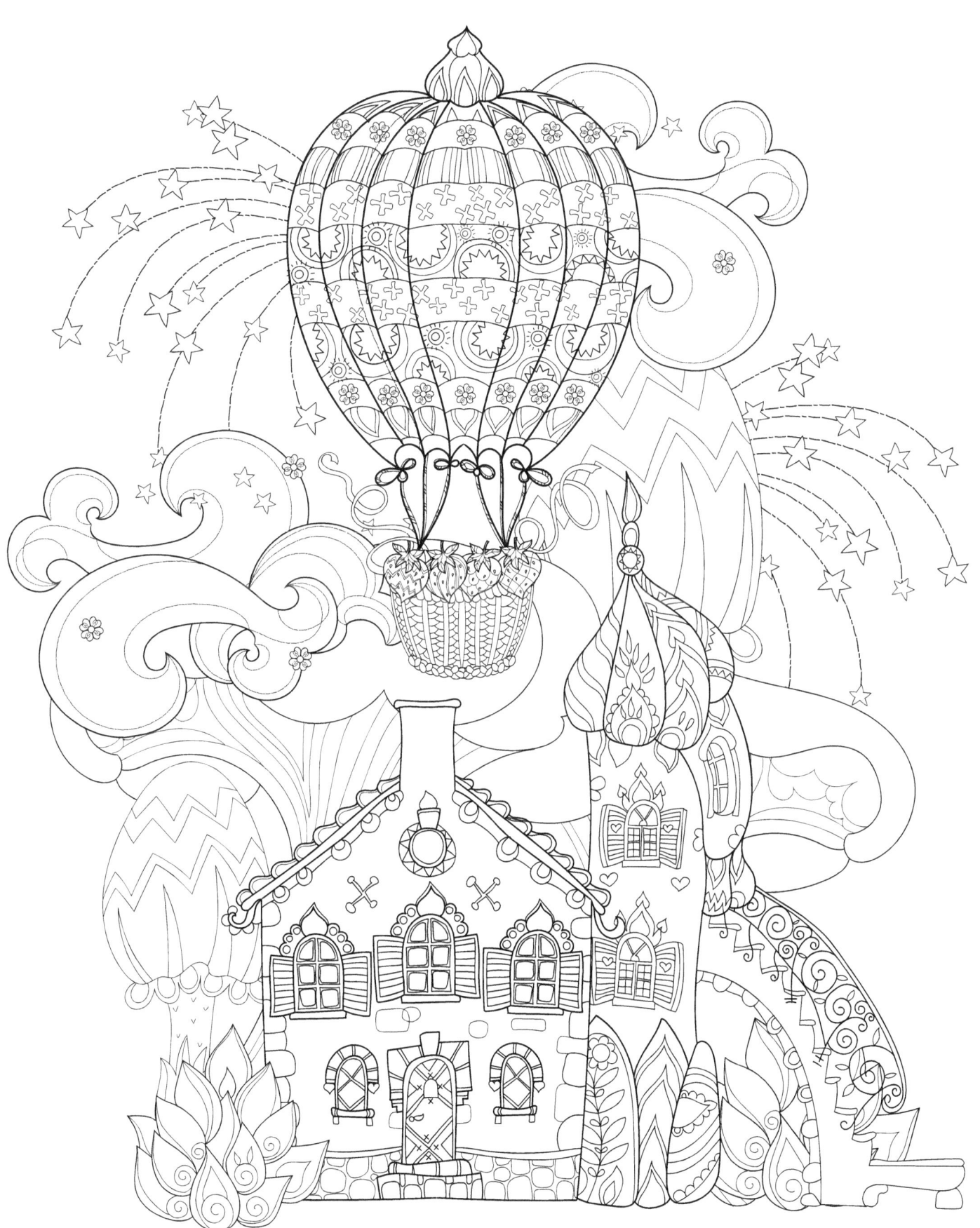

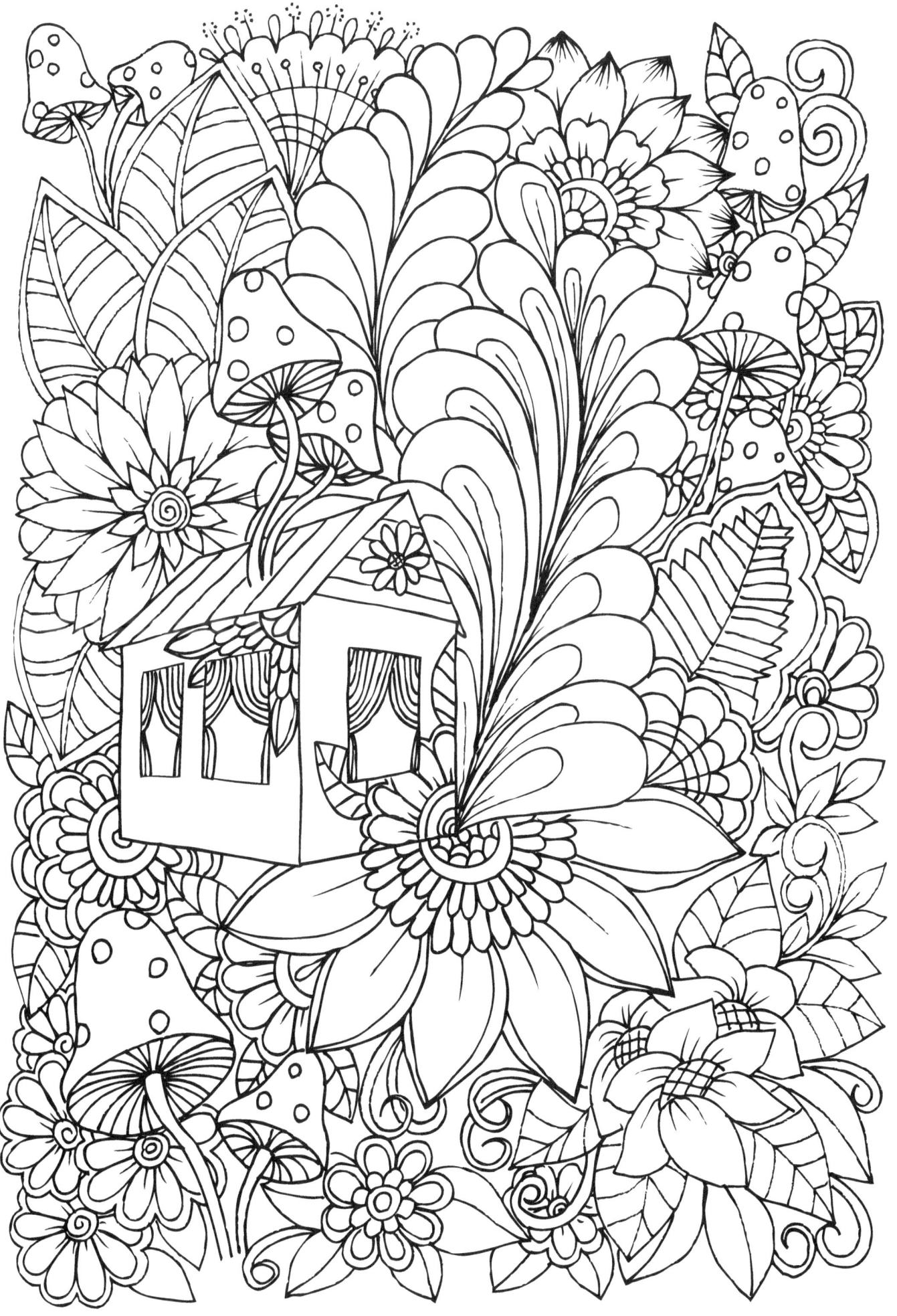

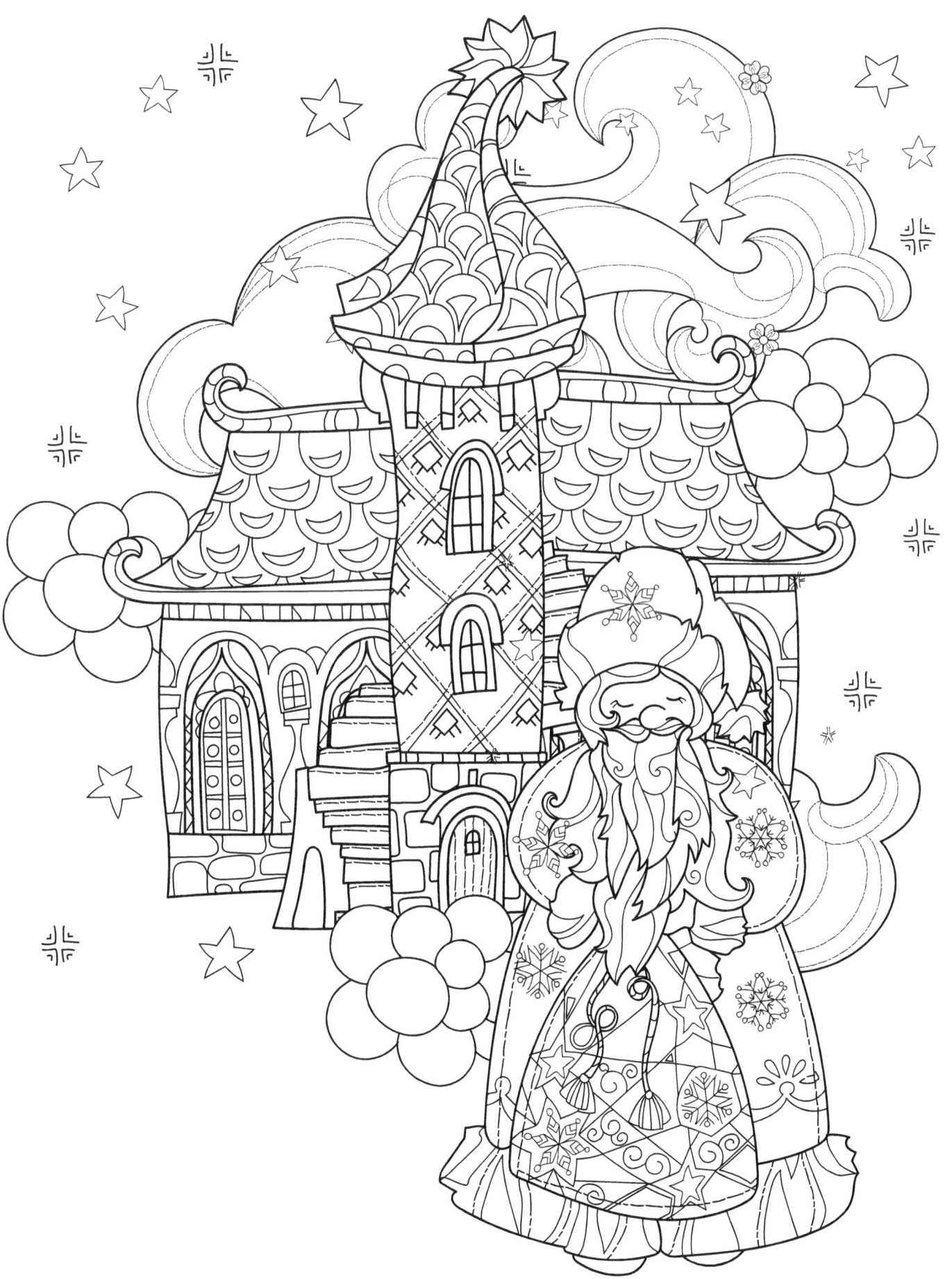

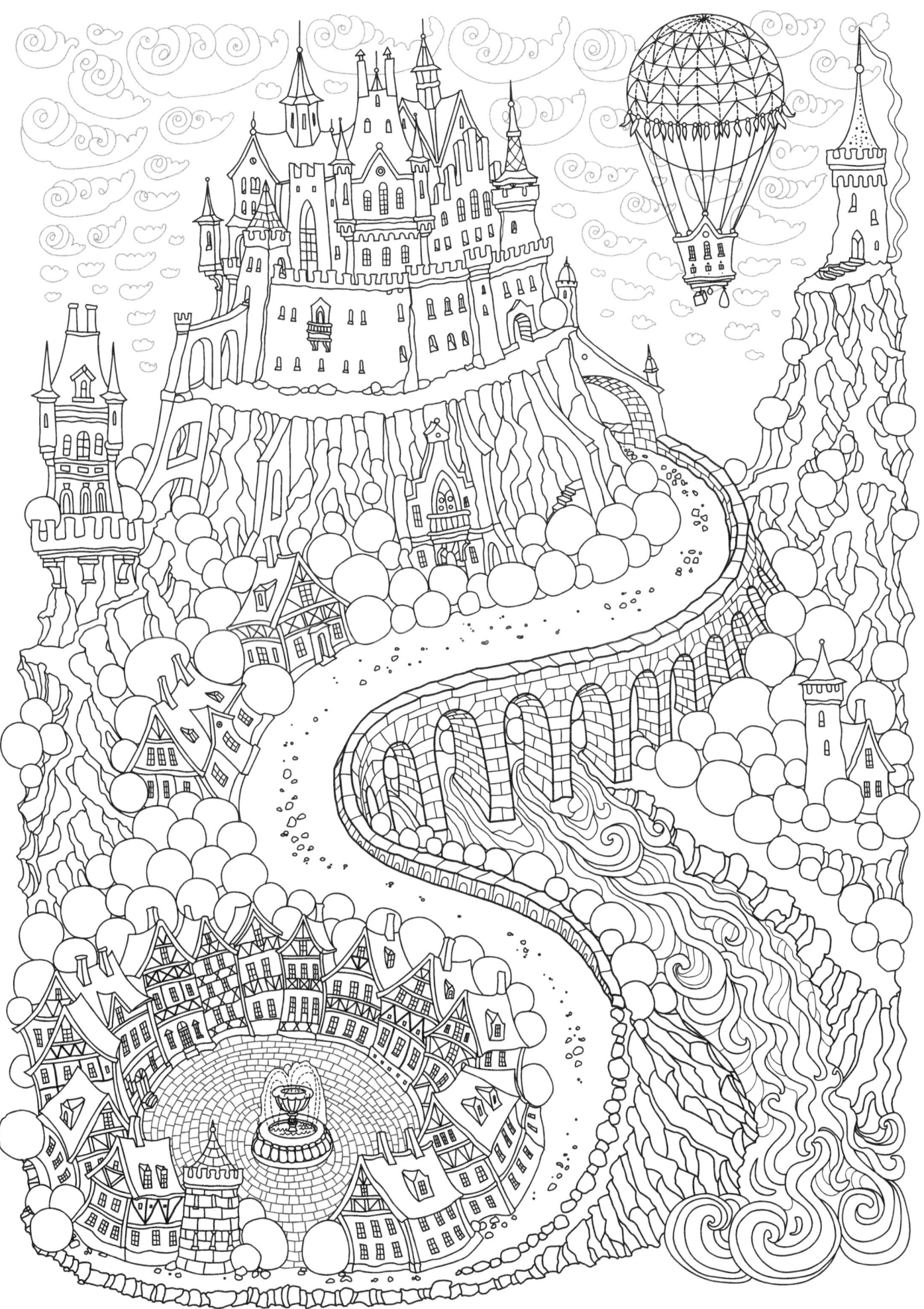

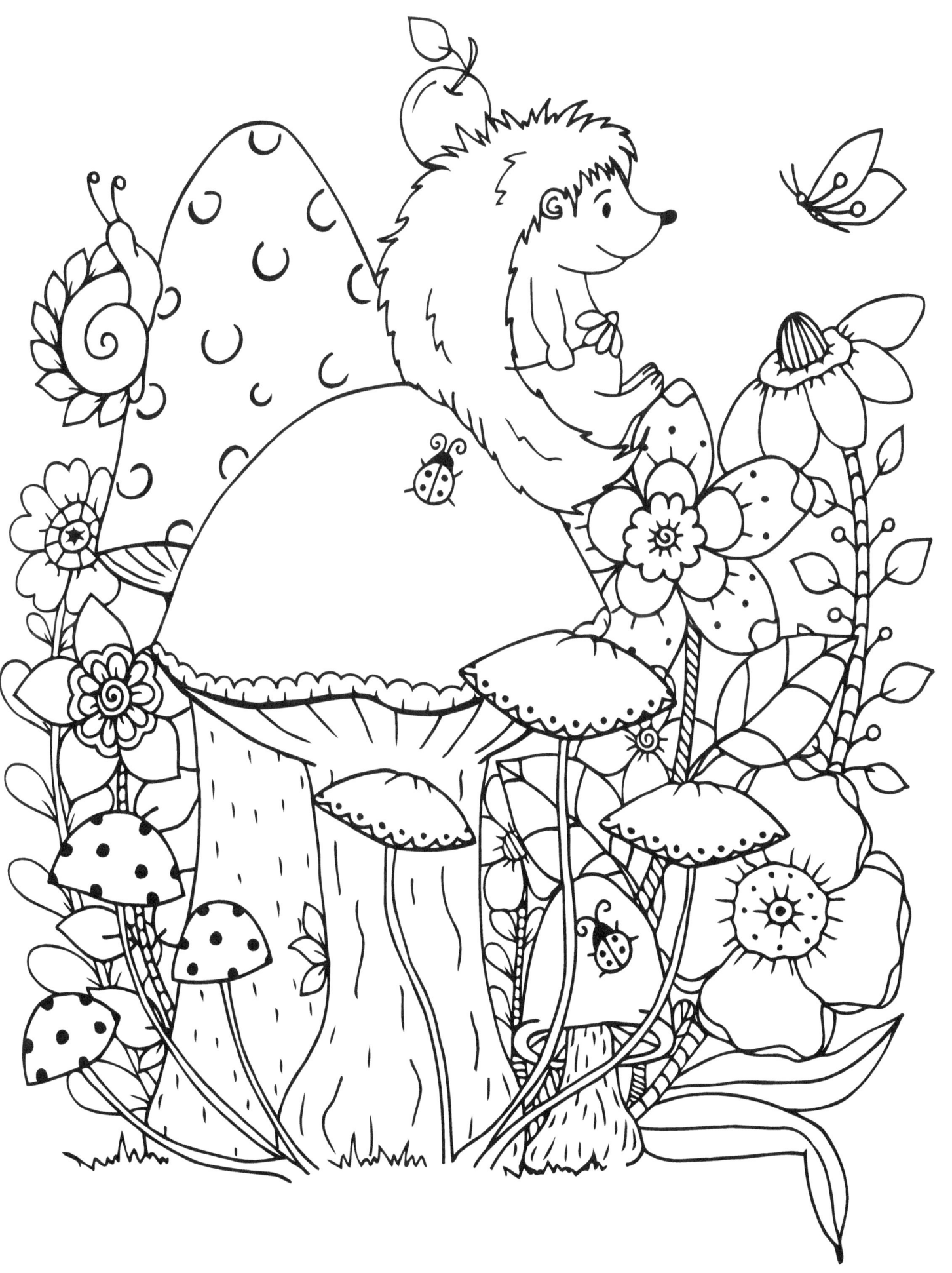

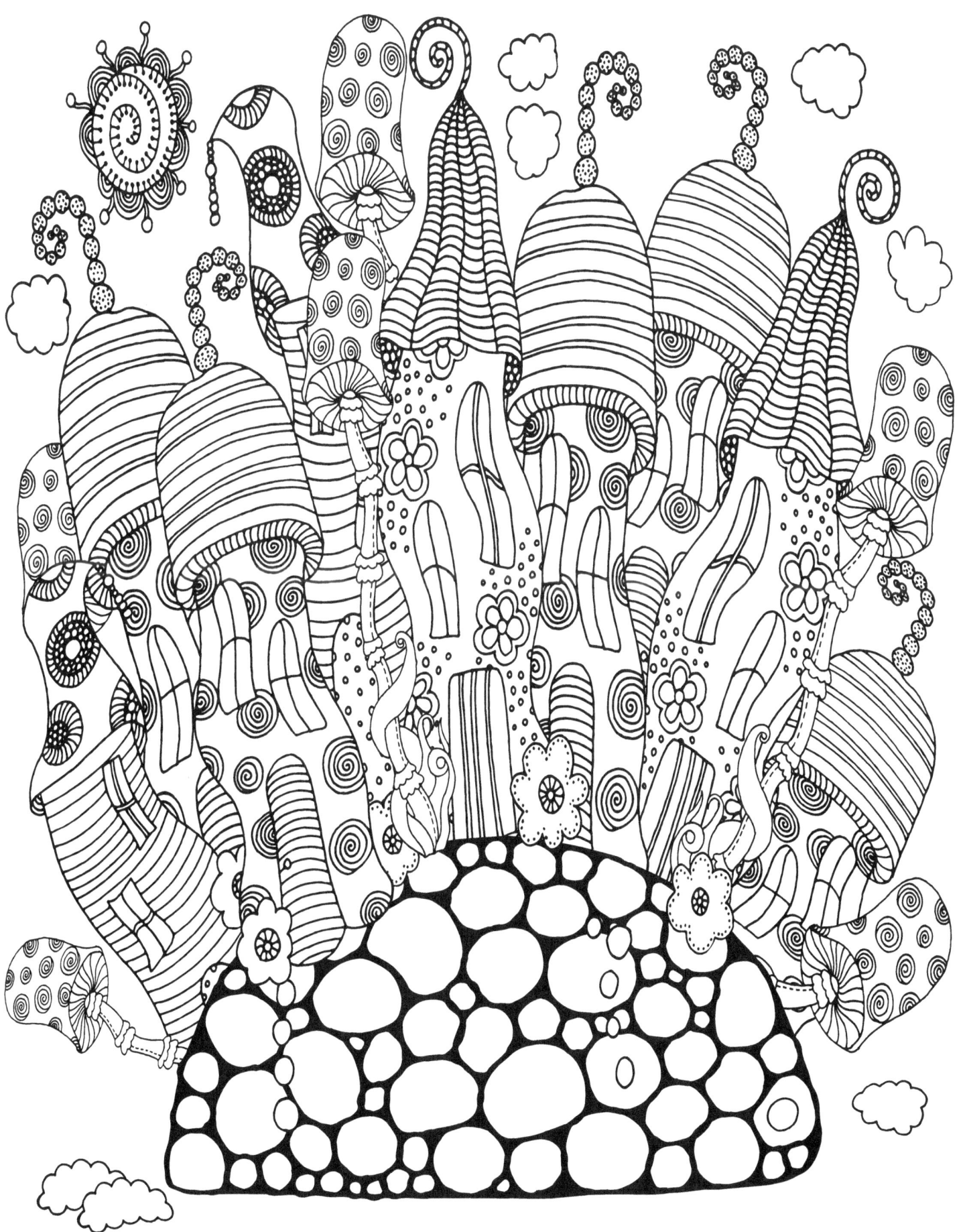

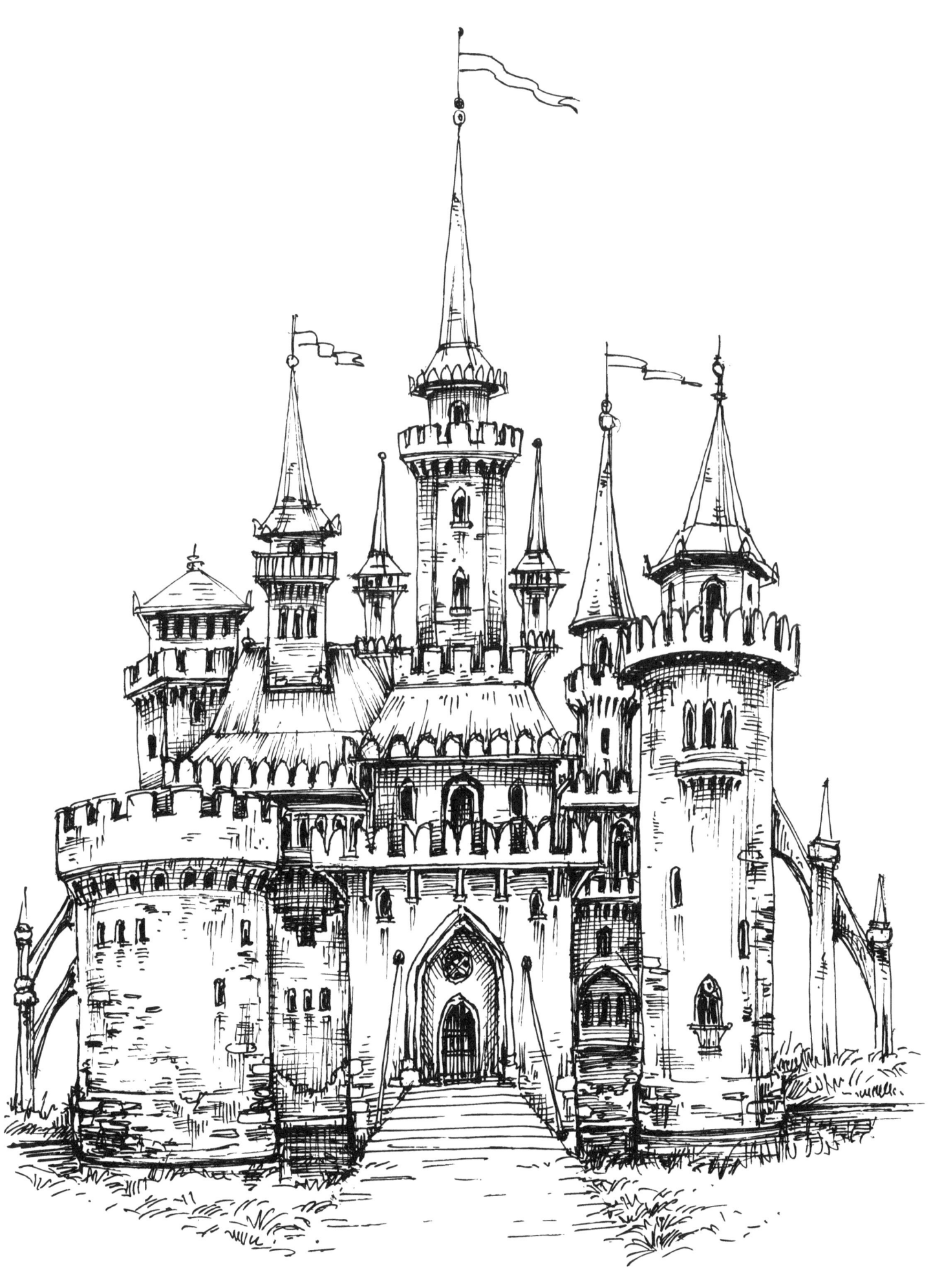

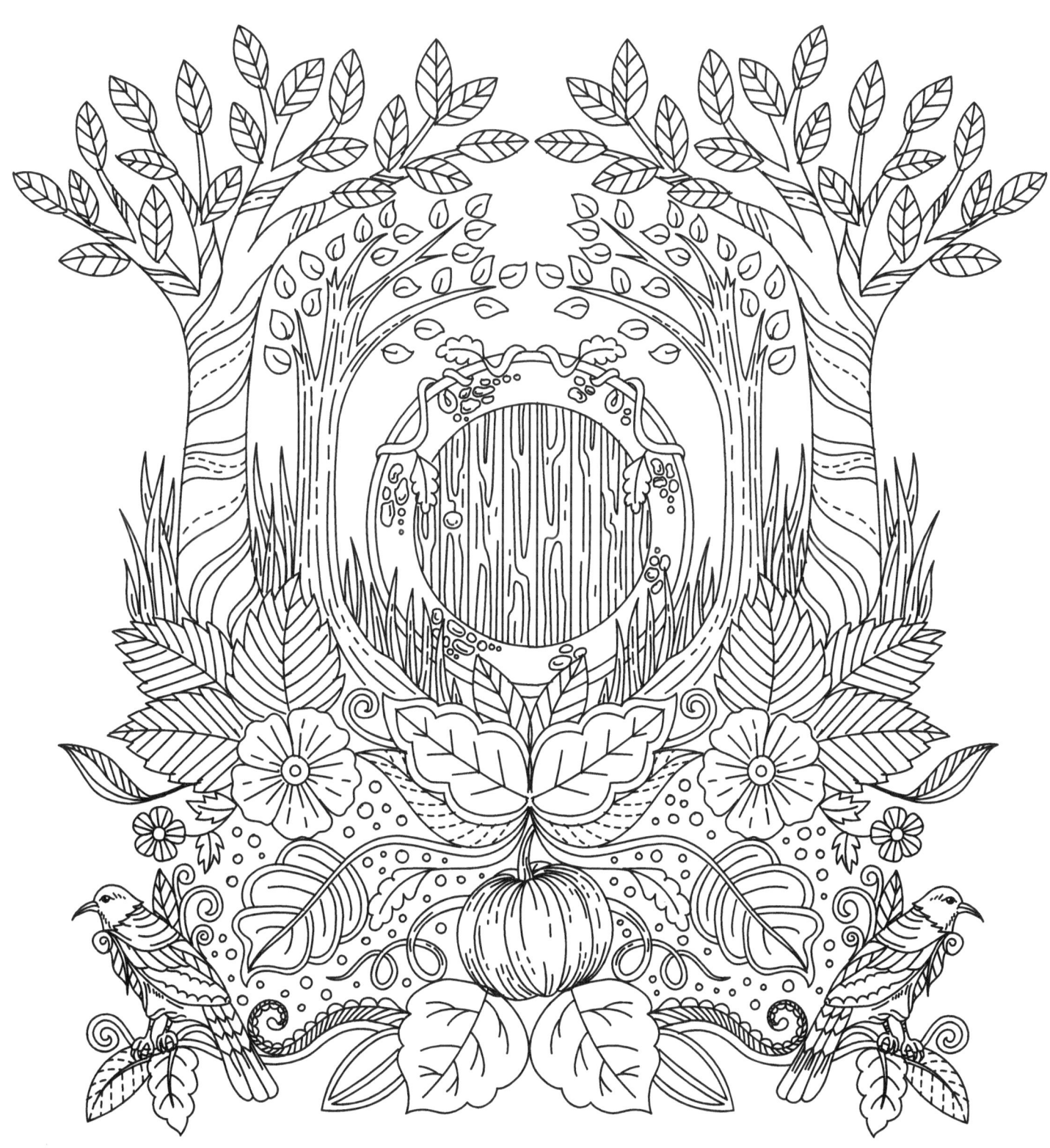

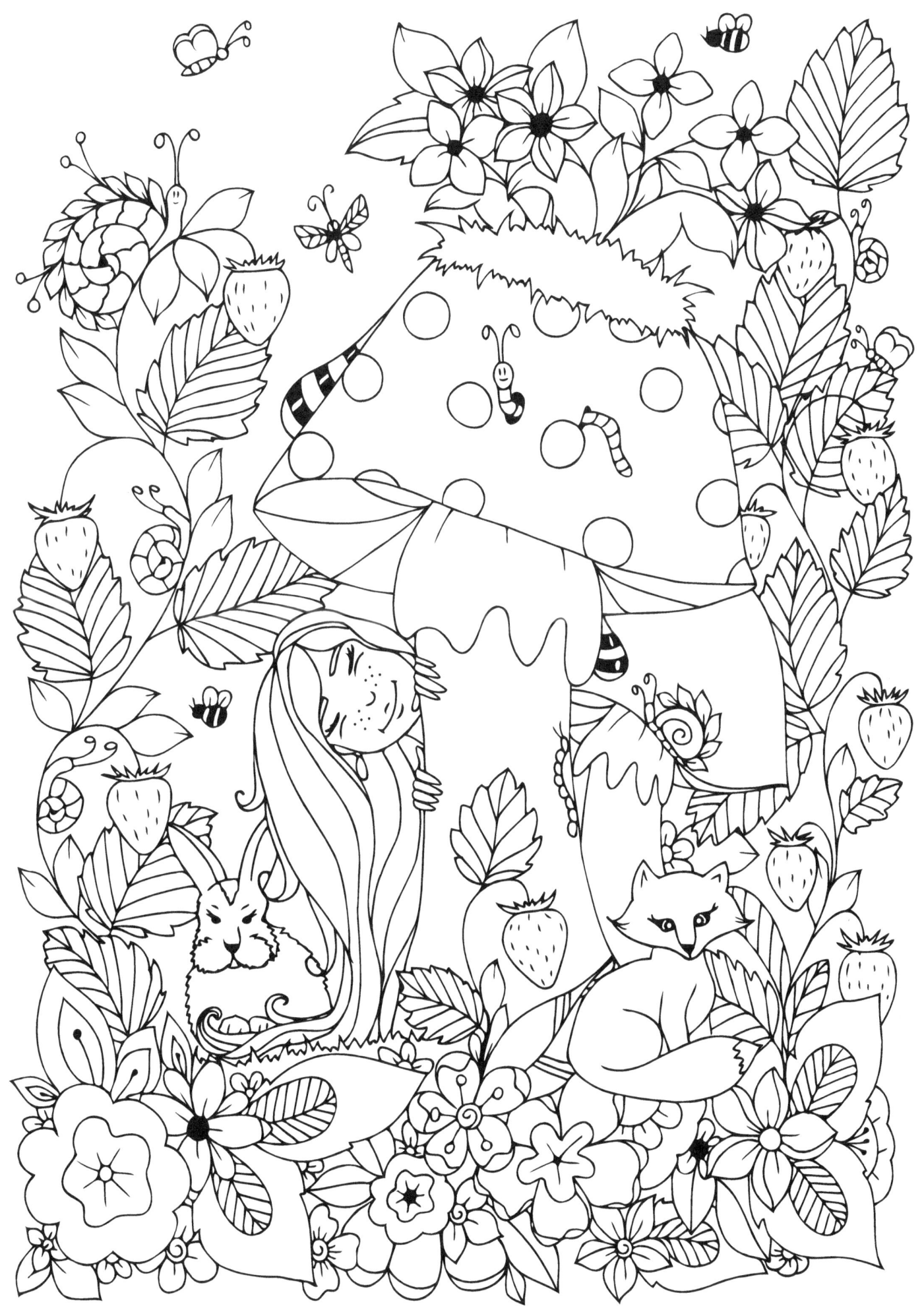

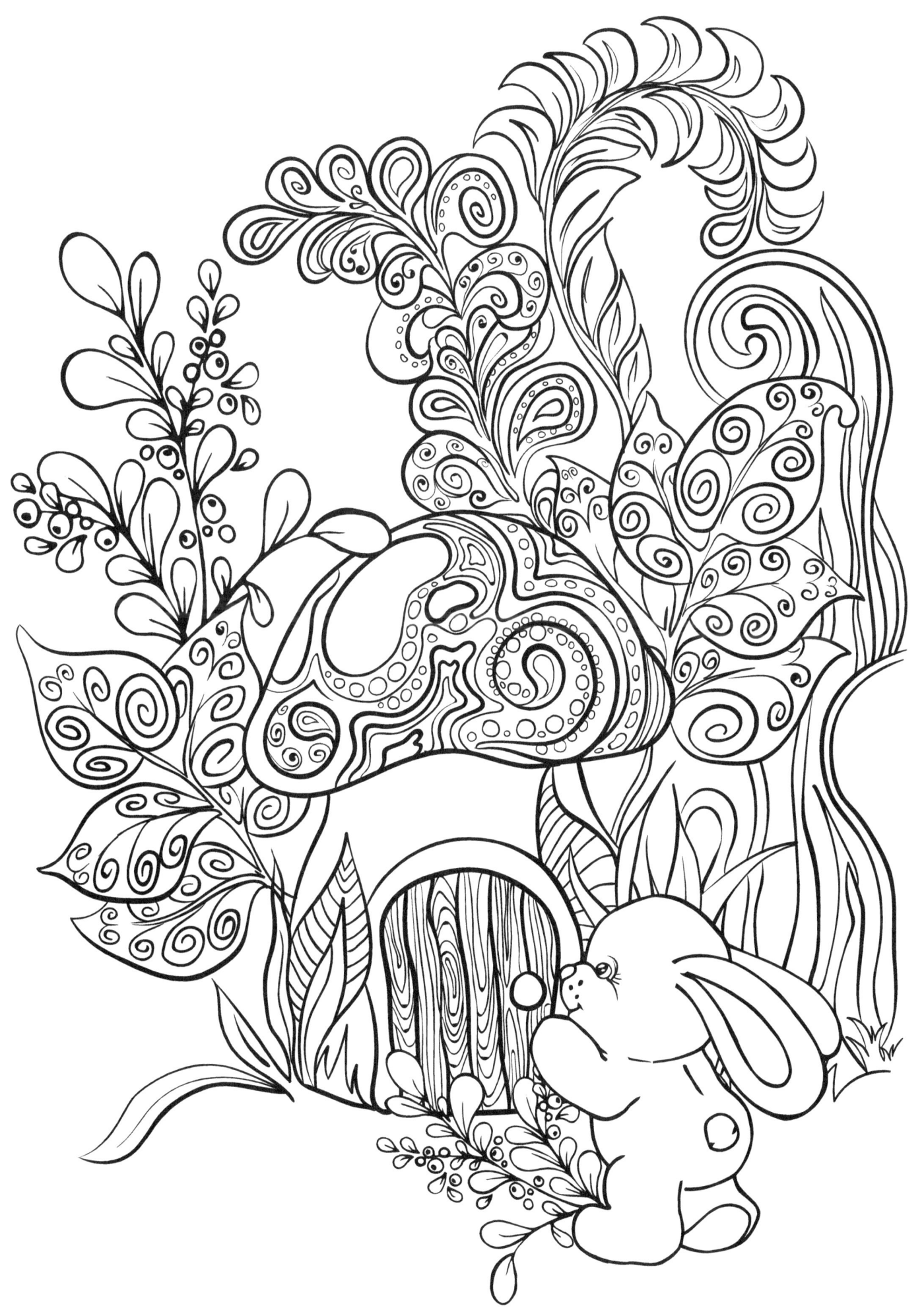

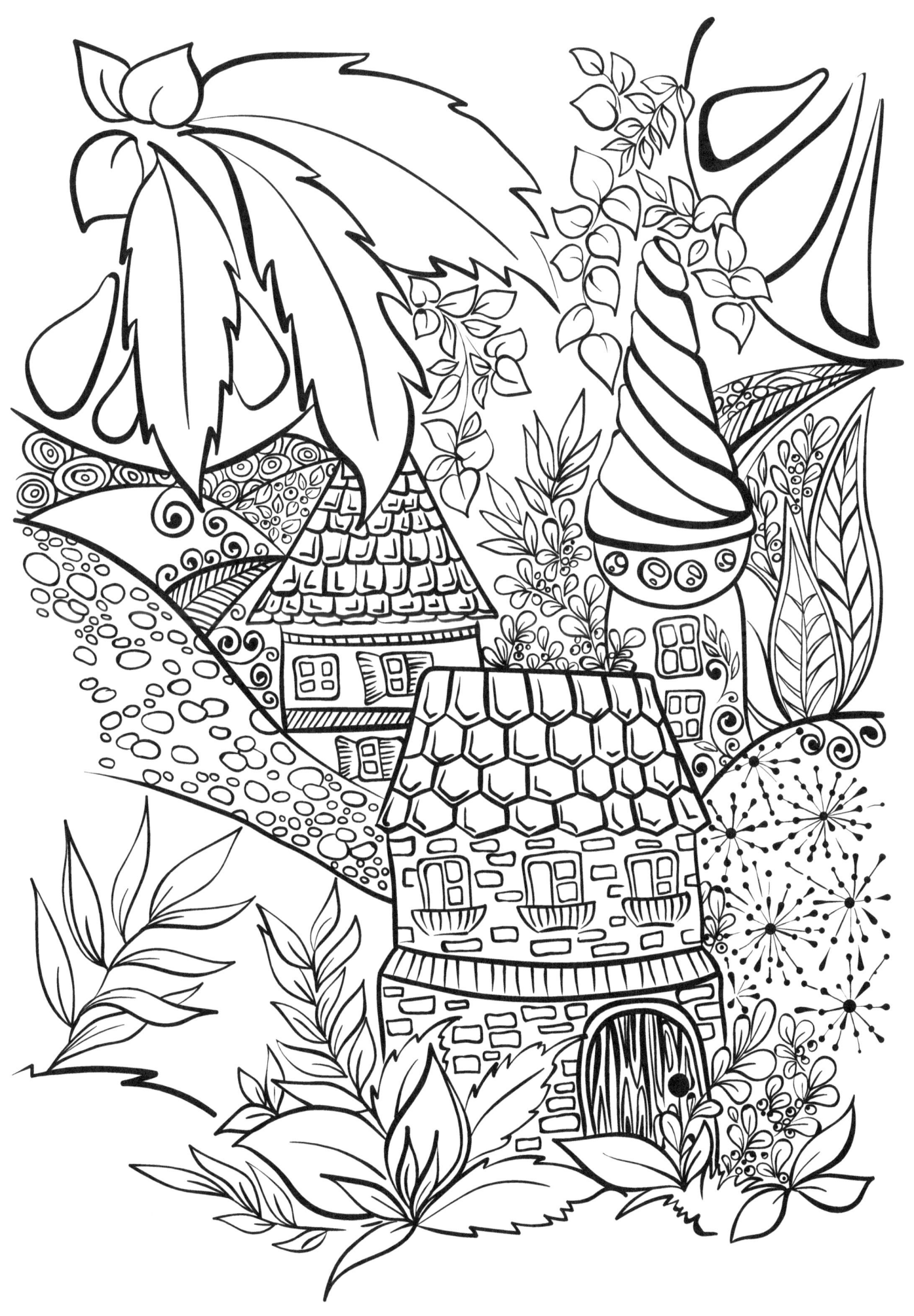

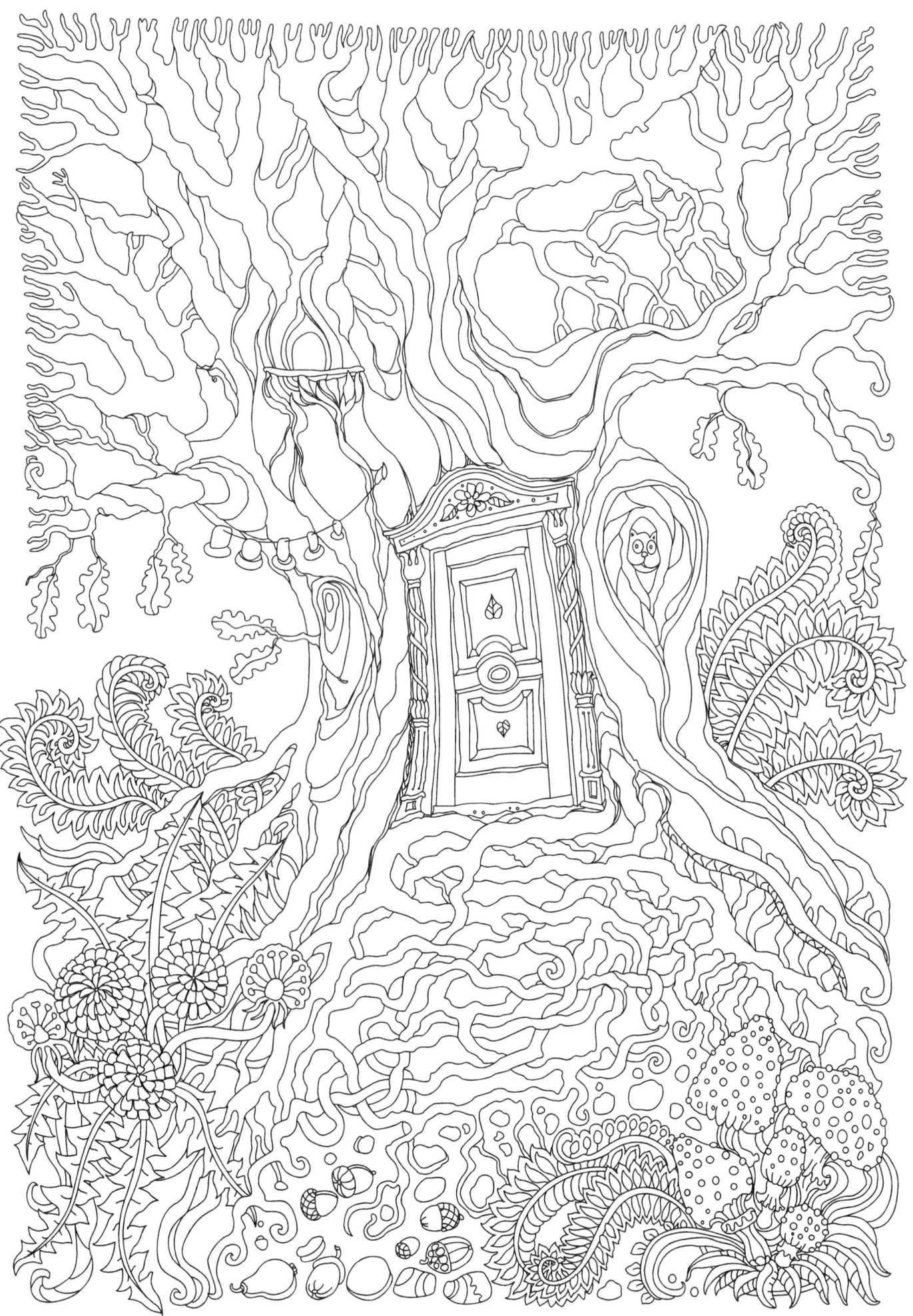

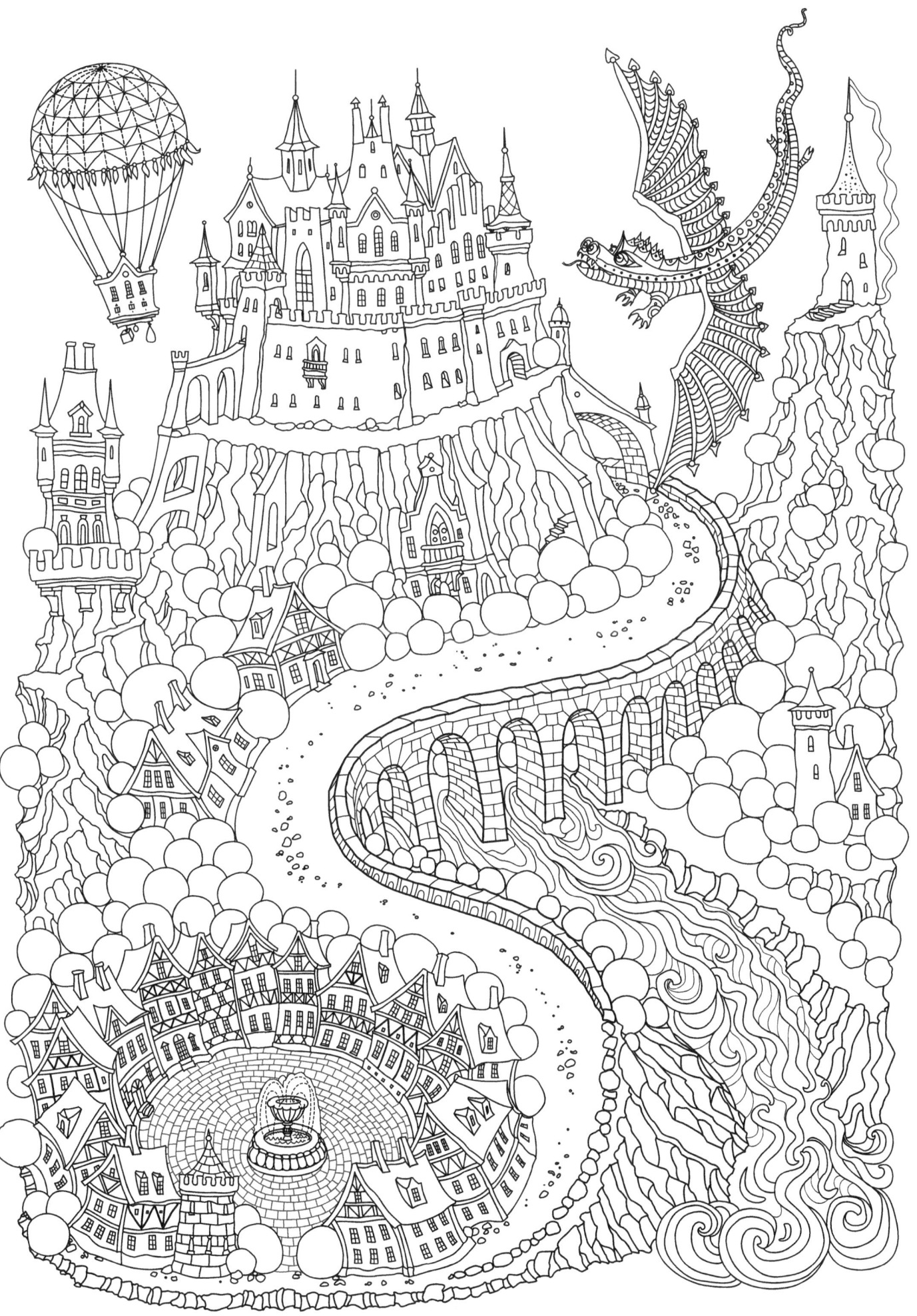

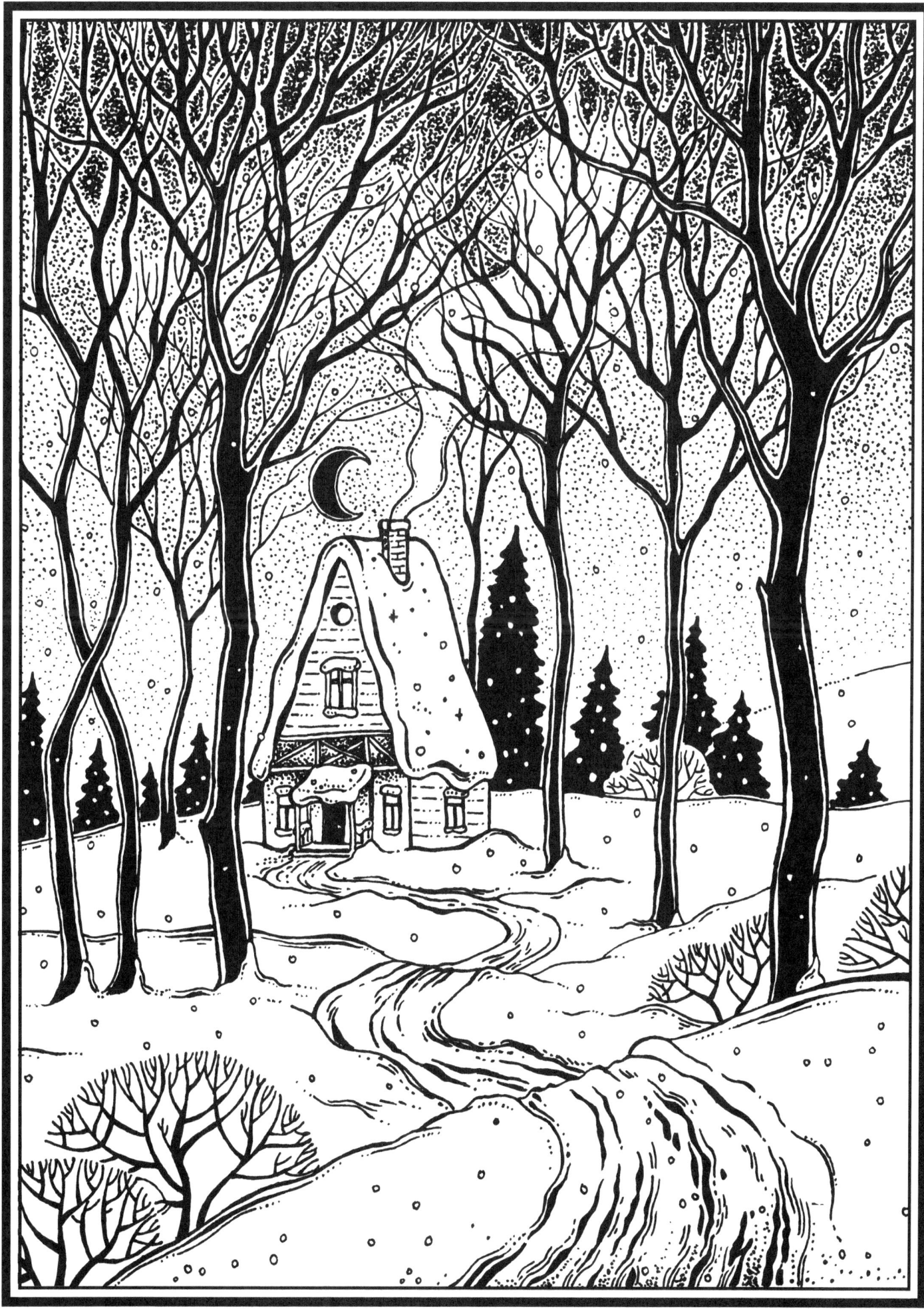

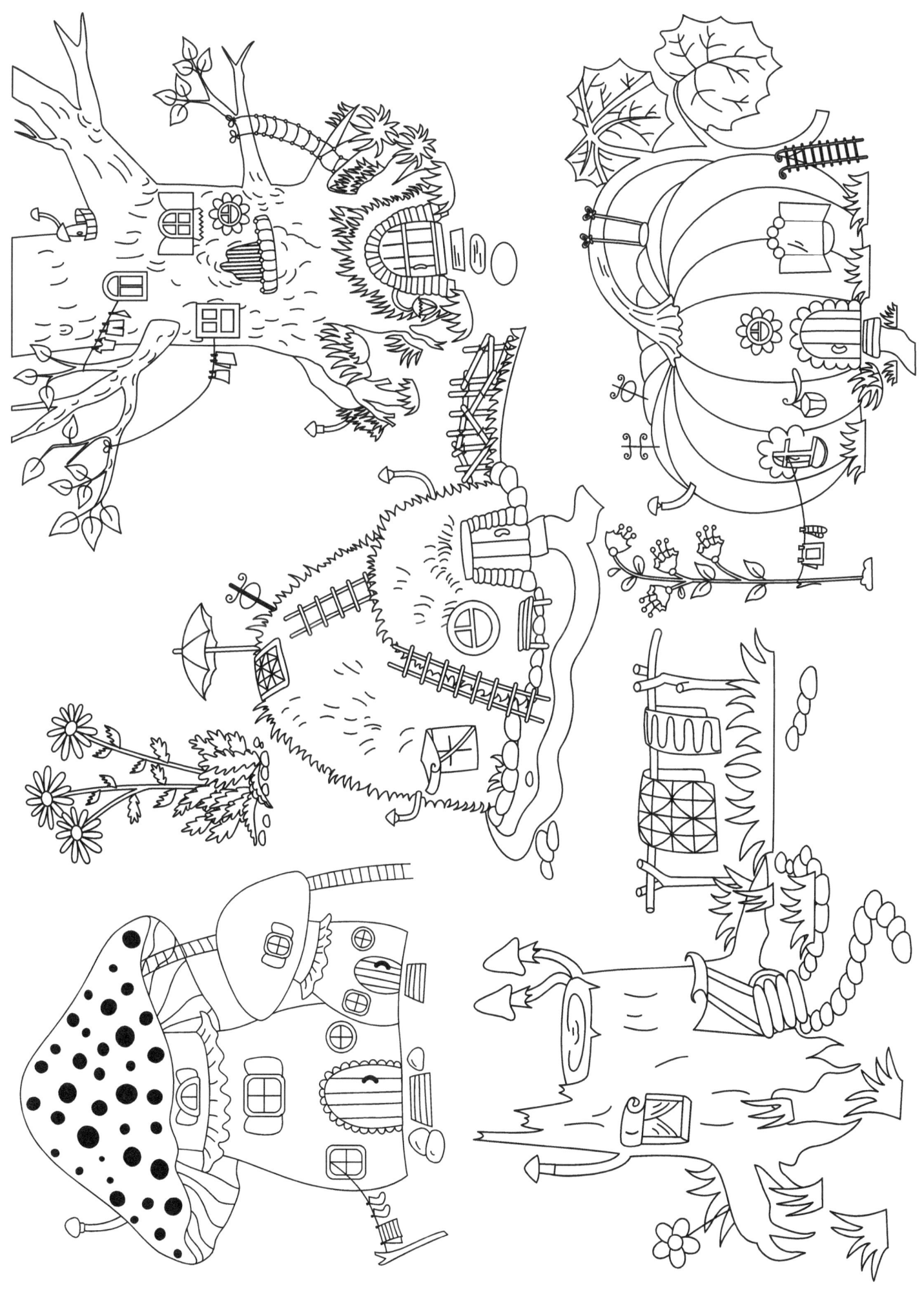

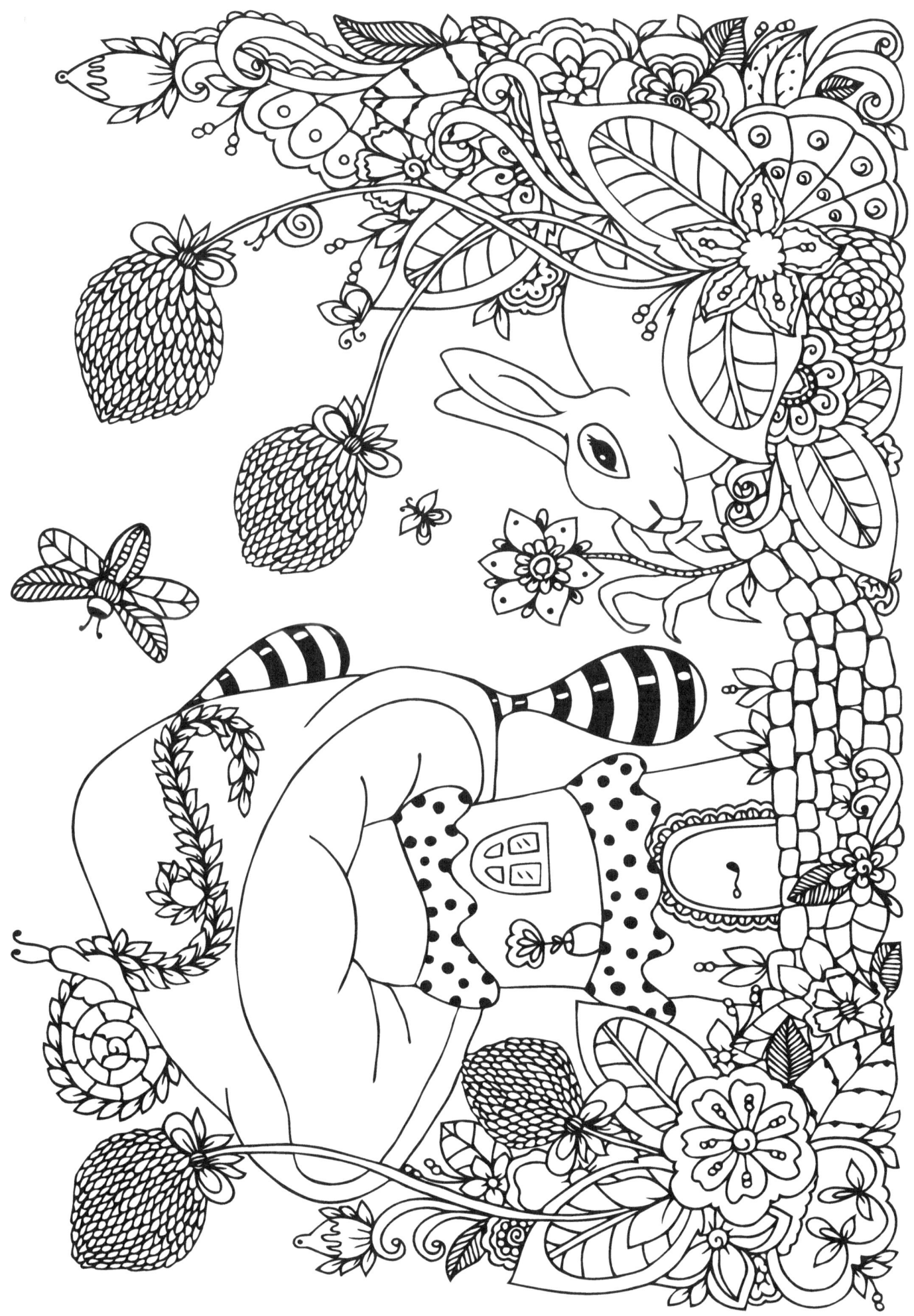

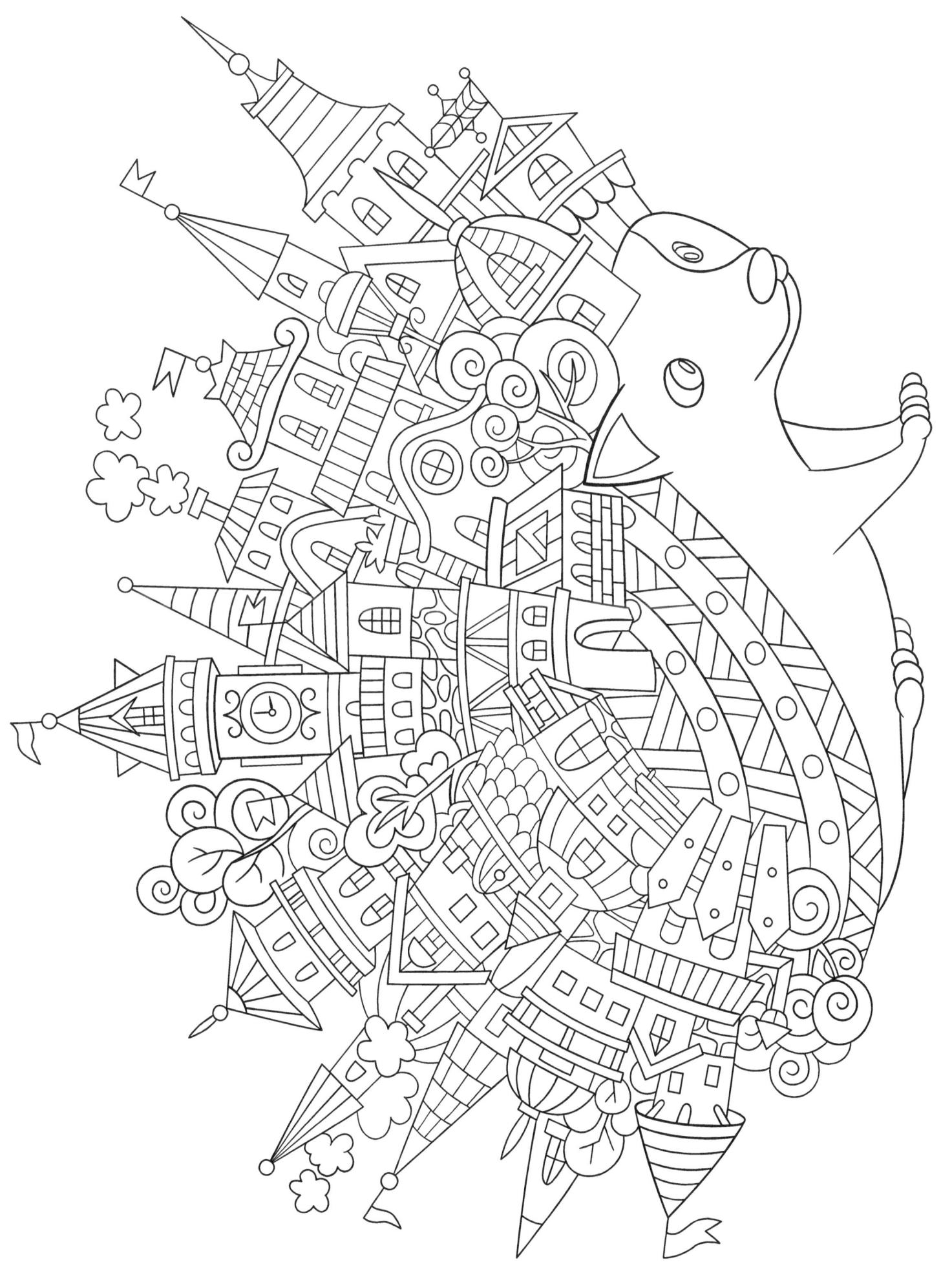

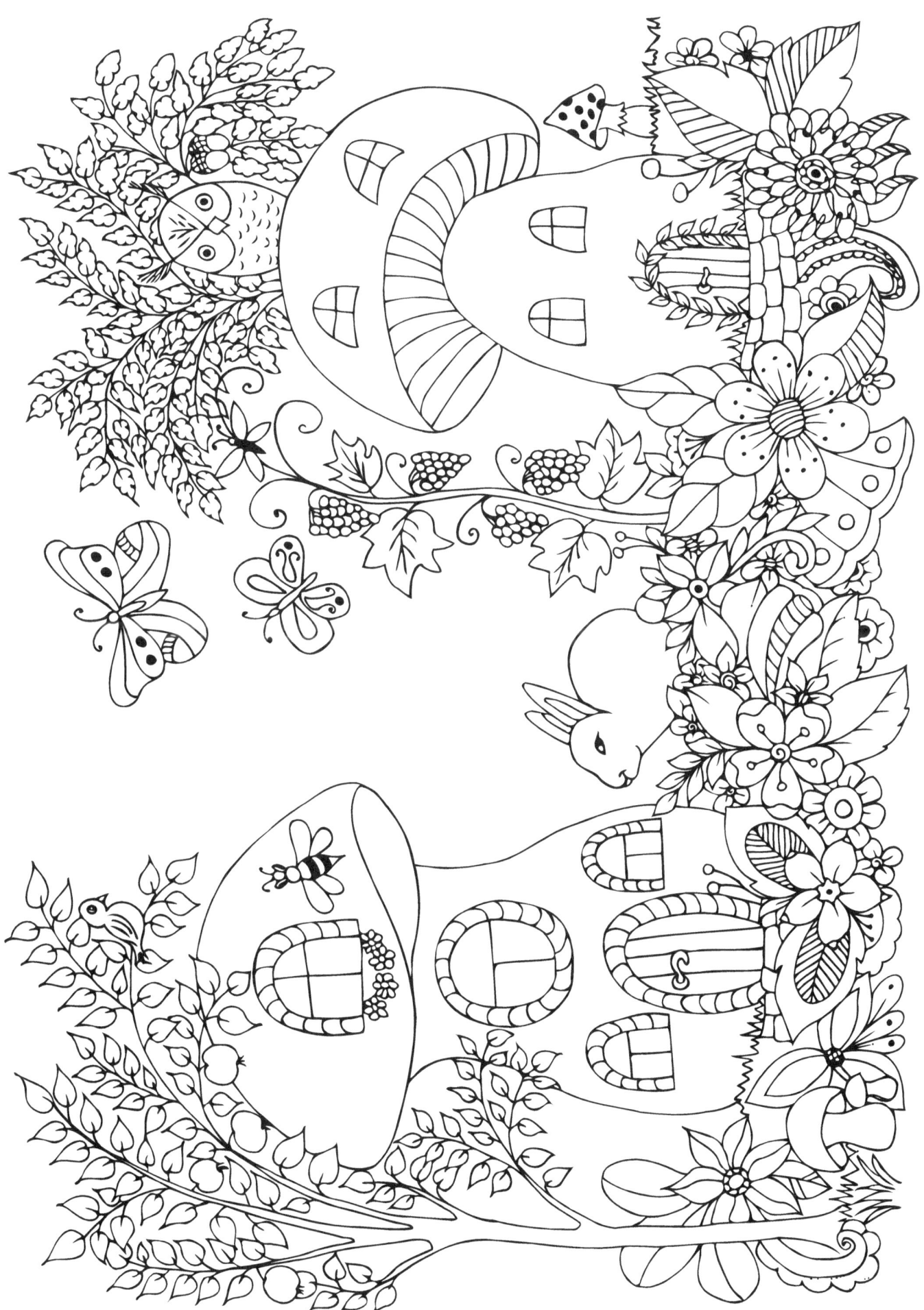

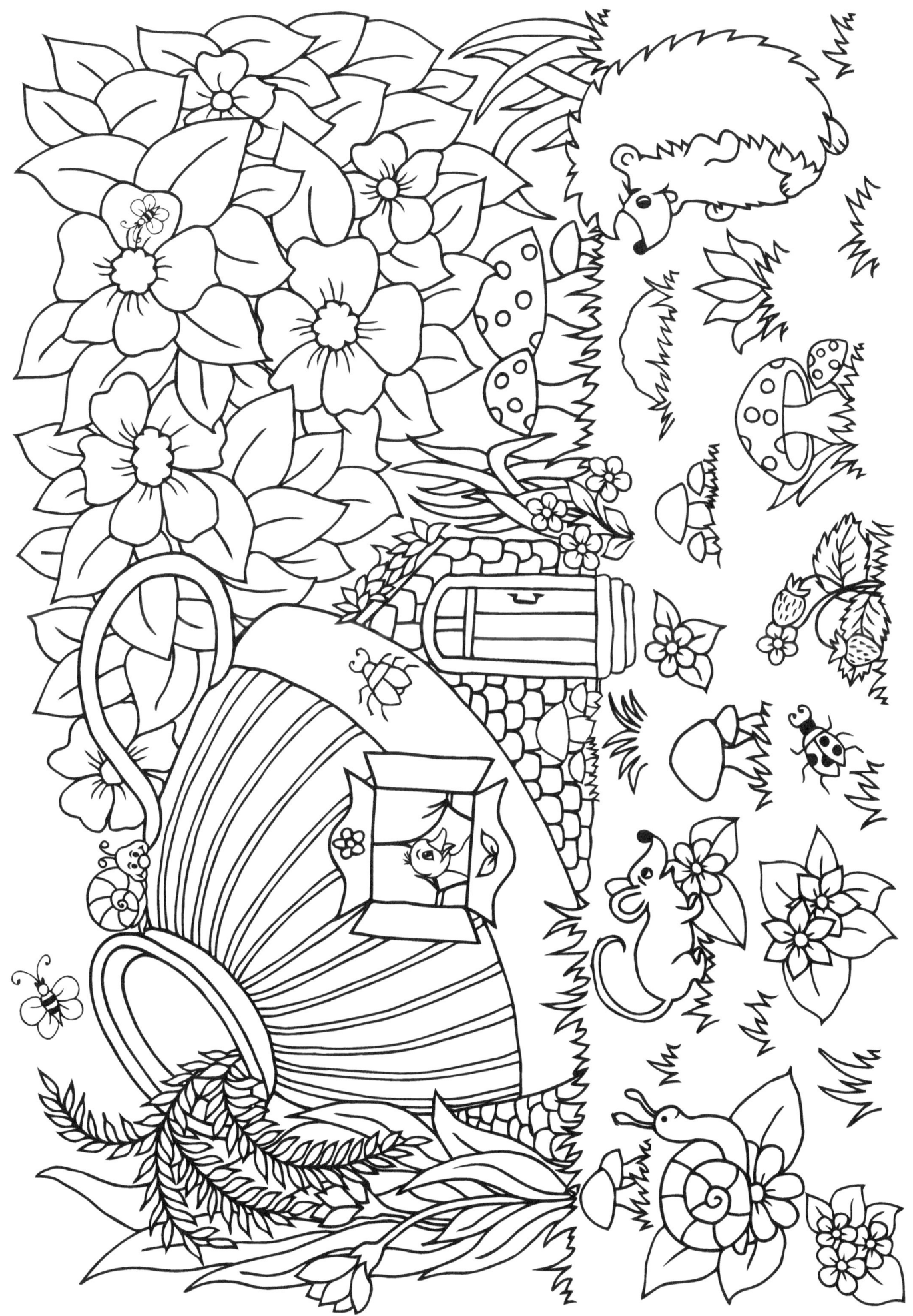

www.ingramcontent.com/pod-product-compliance
Lightning Source LLC
Chambersburg PA
CBHW062334220526
45469CB00008B/2710